COOKIE A

PHOTOGRAPHY BY LAURA KICEY

For my husband who is simply wonderful.

Monkey, Hedera, and Clandestine originally appeared in Knitty. www.knitty.com
Lissajous originally appeared in Twist Collective. www.twistcollective.com

Photography: Laura Kicey
Styling: Sarah Beaver
Production: Kristi Geraci
Book Design: Vanessa Yap-Einbund
Technical Editor: Janice Kang

First published in 2010 by One Leg Press
www.onelegpress.com

ISBN-13: 978-0-9845726-0-1

Printed and bound in China through Asia Pacific Offset.

10 9 8 7 6 5 4 3 2 1

Contents

Introduction

Knitty magazine is where it all began. It was 2005, I was newly married and had moved to California. I had two mismatching socks under my belt and somehow knitting those two socks had given me the confidence and desire to create and explore. Armed with a small arsenal of stitch dictionaries, I set out to design an original sock pattern. It wasn't easy, but I enjoyed playing with the stitches, figuring out how the pattern would come together, and watching the sock take shape on the needles. After I finished the sock, I found myself posed in my wedding dress along a strip of California coast, borrowed mannequin leg in hand. It appeared risqué to onlookers, but the leg was well attired in my hand knit sock creation. That first pattern was Pomatomus, published in the winter 2005 issue of *Knitty*. It was named after the genus of the blue fish because the colorway was a beautiful mix of blue and green, and the details resembled fish scales. It was my first flirtation with sock knitting, and I was in love.

Shortly thereafter, I followed with Hedera, published in the spring 2006 issue of *Knitty*. This time the mannequin leg was posed near a pond in a lush green environment. Then more patterns came, one in each of the next three consecutive issues of *Knitty*, culminating with the enormously popular Monkey pattern (page 60). I was hooked, and based on the thousands of Monkey projects in Ravelry's online knitting database, I wasn't the only one with a monkey on my back.

Pomatomus, 2005

What is it about sock knitting that has captivated so many knitters? Socks are small, portable, and knitted around and around and around. There's something about knitting in circles that is addictive—it's difficult to put down a sock in progress because you're always poised to knit the next step, whatever that may be. The small size is ideal for experimentation with new yarns, new techniques and new constructions. I never would have tried a pattern like Pomatomus on a sweater, but with socks I felt liberated from fear of mistakes or sizing issues. In short, socks are perfect.

Five years later, my love affair with sock knitting is still going strong. I've designed dozens of sock patterns since Pomatomus, and I'm still amazed by new ideas and possibilities I want to try. For this volume I've assembled a dozen previously published patterns and seven brand new patterns. They are arranged in three sections: *Columns*, *Tessellations*, and *Diagonals*. Each section explores an underlying structure for creating patterns within socks. While some of the socks may seem complex, there is always a simple base geometry with textures built on top. Included with each pattern are charts, diagrams, and schematics to act as road maps for your journey through the sock. Despite the hard angles in the underlying structure, the resulting patterns have a more organic feel with curves, florals, twists and turns. I love balancing soft with rigid.

Hedera, 2006

I hope this new vocabulary proves useful when considering how patterns work within the knitted fabric. The progression from *Columns* to *Tessellations* to *Diagonals* builds on increased understanding of the basic structures, and projects are arranged within each chapter in increasing levels of complexity. All of the socks are knitted from the top down and use fingering weight yarn. I've included multiple sizes where possible.

My journey through the world of sock knitting has been a wonderful one, and I hope to help make yours wonderful as well.

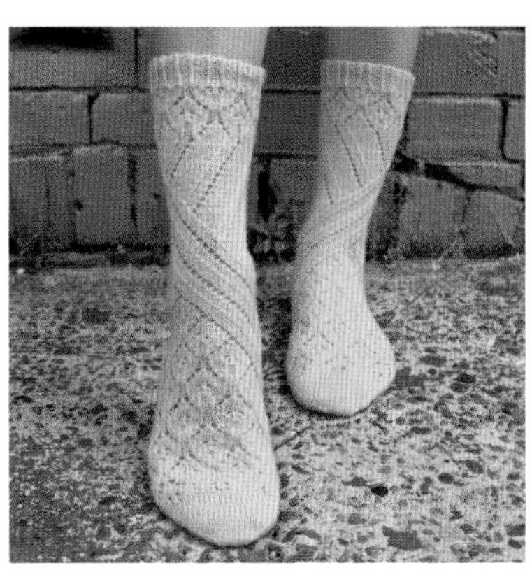

Pointelle, 2010

Laura Kicey

Originally from Lancaster, PA, Laura Kicey is a photographer and graphic designer currently based in Ambler, PA. She received a BFA in Communication Design from Kutztown University, during which time she initially explored black and white film photography. Several years later, she began her digital color photography work, the passion for which grew out of the discovery of the supportive community at flickr.com, an online photo sharing site.

"In my explorations of the world around me, I seek out the literal or figurative underbelly of places and things," says Kicey. "I marvel at the way time, history and nature reform structures and lives, and the secrets and stories forgotten objects can tell. Often the unseen is the most telling and sensitive. Back alleys and abandoned places draw me in. The things I see in these places where I most likely should not be, I take out of their realm and ask the viewer to see what has been missed. I prefer to use what I encounter as I find it, making visual order of chaos by giving new context to what I have singled out."

Kicey's work has appeared in Beyond Architecture: Imaginative Buildings and Fictional Cities (Gestalten) and such periodicals as *JPG, LAB*, *Time Out*, *TECHMAG* and *Nerve*. As a commercial photographer her clients have included Pantone, Urban Outfitters, Terrain and the American Institute of Architects.

Backbone, 2009

Additionally she has exhibited fine art photography in the State Museum of Pennsylvania, The Muse Gallery (Philadelphia), Nexus Gallery (Philadelphia), and Musée de l'Elysée (Lausanne, Switzerland), among other galleries and museums.

"Through my professional work as a graphic designer, my interest and careful study of color and space has been developing over the years; in my photographs, I reapply those ideas to the world as I see it," says Kicey. "My post-processing work is used less to distort or invent, rather more to recapture the feelings of the moment, by altering the color. I prefer to restrict myself to one or two dominating colors in a composition to enhance and orchestrate the mood. The goal of every image is to create an experience that invokes all the senses as intensely as when I capture what is before me. Photography has given me a language to translate all of the ideas and things I have been drawn to ever since I was young."

Atrium, 2008

CHAPTER 1

COLUMNS

Ever since the first knit and purl stitches, vertical design elements have been used in knitting. By repeating one element over and over on top of itself, a vertical panel is created that can go all the way from the top of the leg of the sock down to the toe. These panels can then be placed side by side around the sock in a dazzling number of ways. The edges may be well-defined

Hedera Mona BFF Marilinda

with strong vertical lines separating each panel (Hedera) or they can be subtle with one edge flowing into the adjacent column in a more continuous and connected pattern (Mona). The vertical panels themselves can be simply textured (BFF) or complex twisting elements (Marilinda). All the columns can begin and end at the same spot, or they can be staggered (Stalagmite). Perhaps they travel straight up and down, uninterrupted, or maybe they meet other shapes along the way (Lissajous). An advantage to column patterns is that it's easy to keep track of where you are by double checking that each repeat flows into the one below it. Also, the vertical lines of the ribbing should align with the vertical lines of columns. Though it may be the simplest way to pattern a sock, the variations are endless.

Stalagmite

Lissajous

Lissajous (short version)

Hedera

Named after the leafy plant, these socks are quite elastic for a forgiving fit. The vertical panels are clear to see with a twisted stitch rib separating each vine-like column. The 4-row repeat is easy to memorize and will allow you to see the vertical structure behind this surprisingly simple pattern. Larger sizes are created by adding additional columns to the leg.

1 LEG

Cast on 50 [60, 70, 80] stitches and distribute such that each needle has a multiple of 10 stitches. Being careful not to twist, join for working in the round and mark beginning of round (page 168). Work chart A (page 14) by repeating first 2 rows for 1 inch for cuff and then working 4-row repeat section until piece measures 6 inches from cast-on edge, ending after row 4 of chart.

• **Size XS and M only** Omit last two stitches from the end of the last round. This will center the top of the foot.

2 HEEL FLAP

Divide for heel flap by placing next 25 [31, 35, 41] stitches on hold for top of foot—2 [0, 2, 0] unworked stitches from end of round plus 23 [31, 33, 41] stitches from beginning of round. Heel flap is worked back and forth over previous 25 [29, 35, 39] stitches. Turn work so that wrong side is facing.

Row 1 (wrong side) Slip 1 purlwise with yarn in front, p24 [28, 34, 38], turn.

Row 2 (right side) (Slip 1 purlwise with yarn in back, k1) 12 [14, 17, 19] times, k1, turn.

Repeat last 2 rows until heel flap measures 2 [2¼, 2½, 2½] inches, ending ready to work a right side row.

SIZES
XS [S, M, L] — shown in size S

YARN
Malabrigo Sock Yarn
100% superwash merino wool
440 yards per 100g
1 [1, 1, 2] skein(s) of Lettuce

NEEDLES
US Size 1 / 2.25mm
or size needed to obtain gauge

NOTIONS
Tapestry needle

GAUGE
In stockinette
32 stitches and 48 rows = 4"

In pattern
30 stitches and 46 rows = 4"

MEASUREMENTS

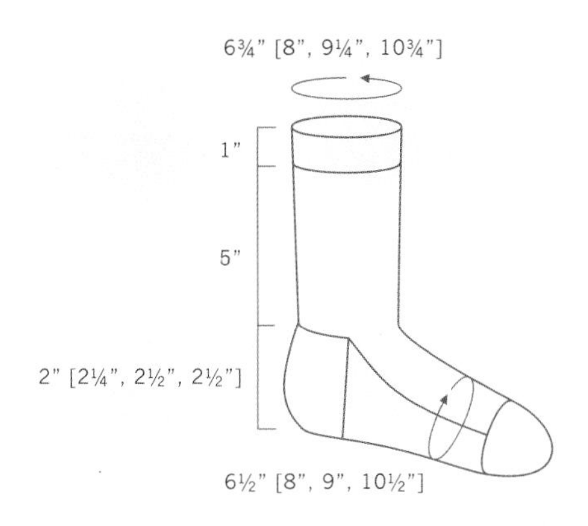

3 TURN HEEL

Continue working back and forth. Use short rows to turn heel as follows:

Row 1 (right side) Slip 1 purlwise with yarn in back, k13 [15, 19, 21], ssk, k1, turn.

Row 2 (wrong side) Slip 1 purlwise with yarn in front, p4 [4, 6, 6], p2tog, p1, turn.

Row 3 Slip 1 purlwise with yarn in back, knit to one stitch before gap caused by turn on previous row, ssk (using one stitch from each side of gap), k1, turn.

Row 4 Slip 1 purlwise with yarn in front, purl to one stitch before gap caused by turn on previous row, p2tog (using one stitch from each side of gap), p1, turn.

Repeat last 2 rows until all heel stitches have been worked, ending ready to work a right side row. 15 [17, 21, 23] heel stitches.

4 FOOT

Resume working in the round as follows: Slip 1 purlwise with yarn in back, k7 [8, 10, 11]. Mark beginning of round. Knit remaining heel stitches, pick up and knit into each slipped stitch along edge of heel flap, make 1, mark right side of foot, work chart B across held stitches, mark left side of foot, make 1, pick up and knit into each slipped stitch along edge of heel flap, knit to end of round.

Right and left side markers divide foot into top of foot section (previously held stitches) and sole. Decrease 2 sole stitches every other round as follows:

Round 1 Knit to 2 stitches before right side of foot, k2tog, work chart B to left side of foot (repeating marked section 2 [3, 3, 4] times), ssk, knit to end of round. 2 stitches decreased.

Round 2 Knit to right side of foot, work chart B to left side of foot, knit to end of round.

Repeat last 2 rounds until 50 [62, 70, 82] stitches remain—25 [31, 35, 41] top of foot stitches and 25 [31, 35, 41] sole stitches.

Continue working even, without decreasing sole stitches, until foot measures 2 inches less than desired length from back of heel turn.

5 TOE

Knit to right side of foot. This is the new beginning of round.

Round 1 Knit to end of round.

Round 2 K1, ssk, knit to 3 stitches before left side of foot, k2tog, k2 (one stitch before and one stitch after left side of foot marker), ssk, knit to 3 stitches before right side of foot, k2tog, k1. 4 stitches decreased.

Repeat last 2 rounds until foot measures desired length, ending after a decrease round. Graft top of foot stitches to sole stitches using Kitchener stitch (page 167). Weave in ends and block.

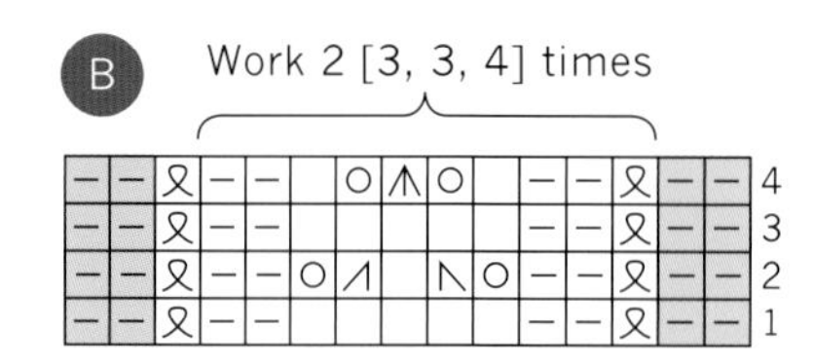

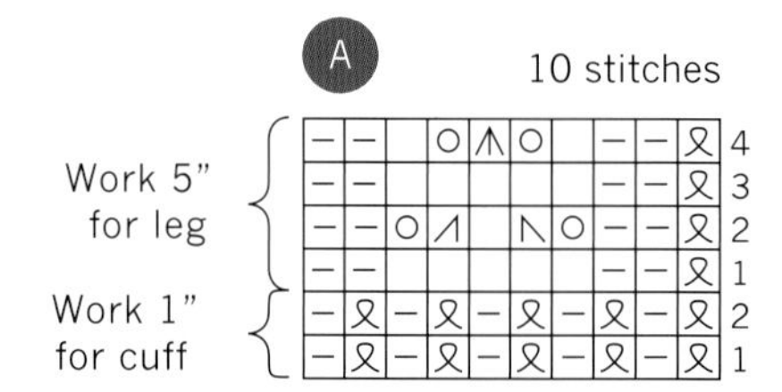

- Knit
- Knit tbl
- Purl
- Yarnover
- K2tog
- Ssk
- Slip 1 knitwise, k2tog, pass slipped stitch over
- Size XS and M only—other sizes ignore these squares.
- • Size XS and M only—omit last two stitches from last round of Leg. They will be used in the top of the foot.

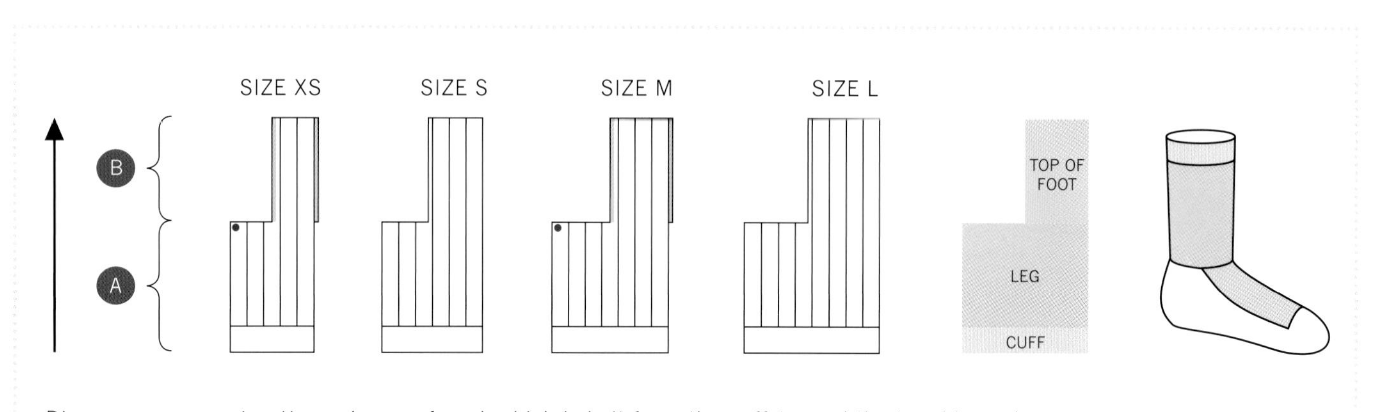

Diagrams represent patterned area of sock which is knit from the cuff toward the toe. Lines show pattern repeats.

Mona

Yarnovers, twisted stitches and directional decreases create this lacy pattern. Each pattern repeat flows from the one below it, and each column melds with its neighbors, creating a harmonious effect. Pay attention to how the pattern begins and where it ends before the heel flap—placements are intentional so that ribbing and heel patterns flow into and out of the main pattern.

1 LEG

Cast on 64 [72] stitches and distribute such that each needle has a multiple of 16 [18] stitches. Being careful not to twist, join for working in the round and mark beginning of round (page 168). Work chart S or L (page 21), depending on size, by repeating first 2 rows for 1 inch for cuff, then working 24-row repeat section until piece measures approximately 6 inches from cast-on edge, ending after row 12 of chart.

2 HEEL FLAP

Divide for heel flap by placing next 31 [35] stitches on hold for top of foot. Heel flap is worked back and forth over remaining 33 [37] stitches. Turn work so that wrong side is facing.

Row 1 (wrong side) Slip 1 purlwise with yarn in front, (p1 tbl, k1) 15 [17] times, p1 tbl, p1, turn.

Row 2 (right side) Slip 1 purlwise with yarn in back, (k1 tbl, p1) 15 [17] times, k1 tbl, k1, turn.

Repeat last 2 rows until heel flap measures 2¼ [2½] inches, ending ready to work a right side row.

3 TURN HEEL

Continue working back and forth. Use short rows to turn heel as follows:

Row 1 (right side) Slip 1 purlwise with yarn in back, k17 [19], ssk, k1, turn.

SIZES
S [L] — shown in size S

YARN
Hazel Knits Artisan Sock
90% superwash merino wool / 10% nylon
400 yards per 120g
1 skein of Blue Jay

NEEDLES
US Size 1 / 2.25mm
or size needed to obtain gauge

NOTIONS
Tapestry needle

GAUGE
In stockinette
32 stitches and 48 rows = 4"

In pattern
32 stitches and 48 rows = 4"

MEASUREMENTS

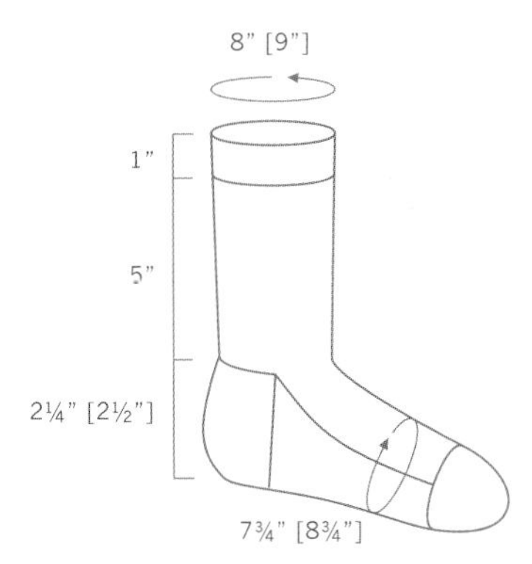

Row 2 (wrong side) Slip 1 purlwise with yarn in front, p4, p2tog, p1, turn.

Row 3 Slip 1 purlwise with yarn in back, knit to one stitch before gap caused by turn on previous row, ssk (using one stitch from each side of gap), k1, turn.

Row 4 Slip 1 purlwise with yarn in front, purl to one stitch before gap caused by turn on previous row, p2tog (using one stitch from each side of gap), p1, turn.

Repeat last 2 rows until all heel stitches have been worked, ending ready to work a right side row. 19 [21] heel stitches.

4 FOOT

Resume working in the round as follows: Slip 1 purlwise with yarn in back, k9 [10]. Mark beginning of round. Knit remaining heel stitches, pick up and knit into each slipped stitch along edge of heel flap, make 1, mark right side of foot, work in established pattern across held stitches (resuming chart on row 13 and omitting last stitch of second repeat of chart), mark left side of foot, make 1, pick up and knit into each slipped stitch along edge of heel flap, knit to end of round.

Right and left side markers divide foot into top of foot section (previously held stitches) and sole. Decrease 2 sole stitches every other round as follows:

Round 1 Knit to 2 stitches before right side of foot, k2tog, work in established pattern to left side of foot, ssk, knit to end of round. 2 stitches decreased.

Round 2 Knit to right side of foot, work in established pattern to left side of foot, knit to end of round.

Repeat last 2 rounds until 62 [70] stitches remain—31 [35] top of foot stitches and 31 [35] sole stitches.

Continue working even, without decreasing sole stitches, until foot measures 2 inches less than desired length from back of heel turn.

5 TOE

Knit to right side of foot. This is the new beginning of round.

Work purl ridge across top of foot as follows: Purl to left side of foot, knit to end of round.

Round 1 Knit to end of round.

Round 2 K1, ssk, knit to 3 stitches before left side of foot, k2tog, k2 (one stitch before and one stitch after left side of foot marker), ssk, knit to 3 stitches before right side of foot, k2tog, k1. 4 stitches decreased.

Repeat last 2 rounds until foot measures desired length, ending after a decrease round. Graft top of foot stitches to sole stitches using Kitchener stitch (page 167). Weave in ends and block.

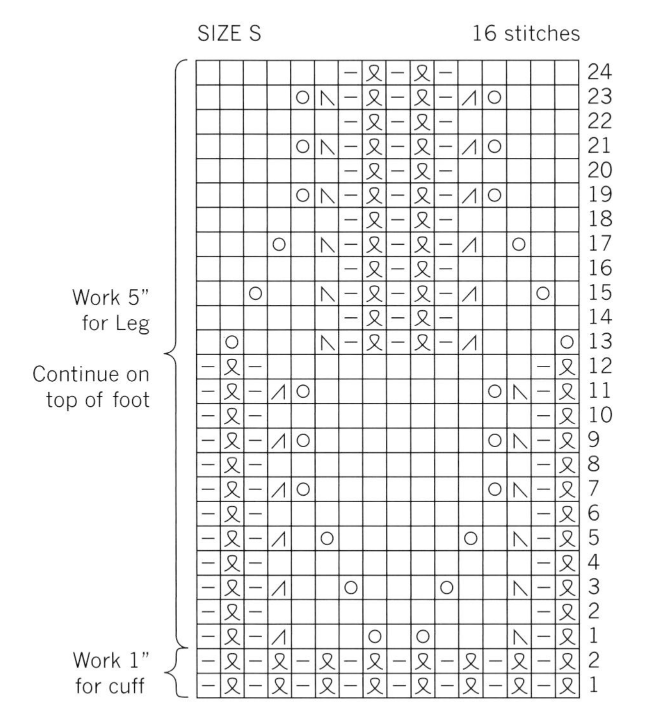

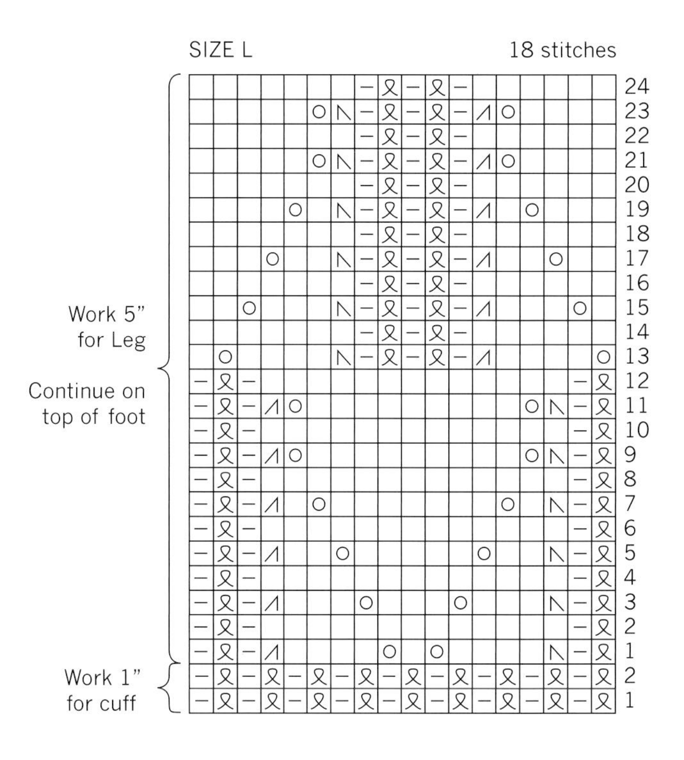

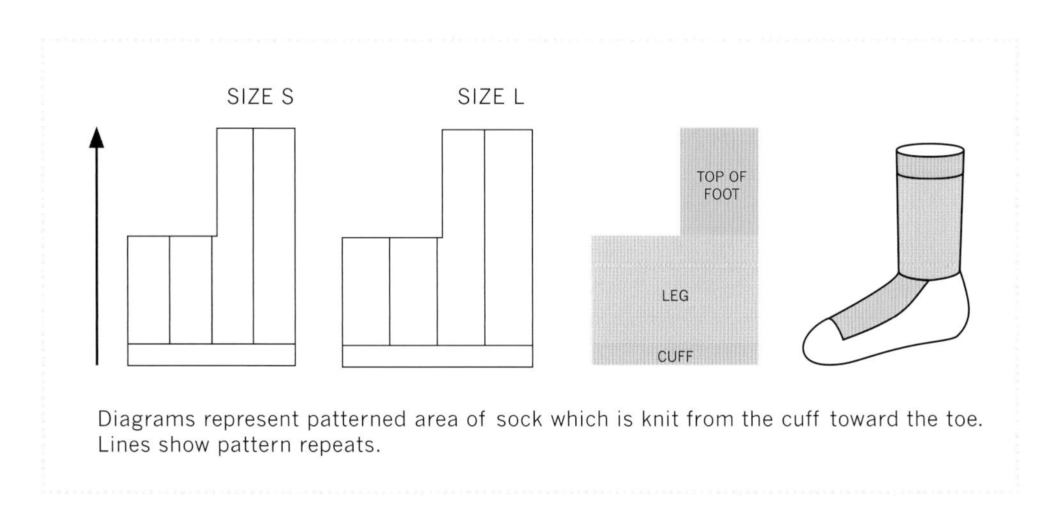

Knit

Knit tbl

Purl

K2tog

Ssk

Yarnover

Diagrams represent patterned area of sock which is knit from the cuff toward the toe. Lines show pattern repeats.

BFF

I originally knit a pair of these socks for my Best Friend Forever (BFF), hence the name. The cables and ribs are wonderfully cozy and make the perfect gift. To compensate for the change in gauge between the cabled and plainer sections, increases and decreases are hidden within the cables to smooth the transition. Like Hedera, the columns in these socks are distinctly separated.

1 LEG

Cast on 56 [64, 72, 80] stitches and distribute such that each needle has a multiple of 8 stitches. Being careful not to twist, join for working in the round and mark beginning of round (page 168). Work chart A (page 26) by repeating first 2 rows for 1 inch for cuff, then working set-up row, increasing to 70 [80, 90, 100] stitches, and then working 6-row repeat section until piece measures approximately 6 inches from cast-on edge, ending after row 6 of chart.

2 SET UP FOR HEEL FLAP

Work chart B, repeating first marked section 4 [4, 5, 5] times, then second marked section 3 [4, 4, 5] times. 62 [72, 80, 90] stitches.

Sizes XS and M only Two stitches are worked beyond the end of the round to center the top of the foot.

3 HEEL FLAP

Divide for heel flap by placing previous 34 [40, 44, 50] stitches—2 [0, 2, 0] stitches just worked plus 32 [40, 42, 50] stitches from end of previous round—on hold for top of foot. Heel flap is worked back and forth over remaining 28 [32, 36, 40] stitches.

Row 1 (right side) (Slip 1 purlwise with yarn in back, k1) 14 [16, 18, 20] times, turn.

Row 2 (wrong side) Slip 1 purlwise with yarn in front, p27 [31, 35, 39], turn.

Repeat last 2 rows until heel flap measures 2 [2¼, 2½, 2½] inches, ending ready to work a right side row.

SIZES
XS [S, M, L] — shown in size S

YARN
Fortissima Socka Color
75% superwash wool / 25% nylon
229 yards per 50g
2 [2, 3, 3] skeins of Light Blue #1004

NEEDLES
US Size 1 / 2.25mm
or size needed to obtain gauge

NOTIONS
Cable needle, tapestry needle

GAUGE
In stockinette
32 stitches and 48 rows = 4"

In pattern
40 stitches and 48 rows = 4"

MEASUREMENTS

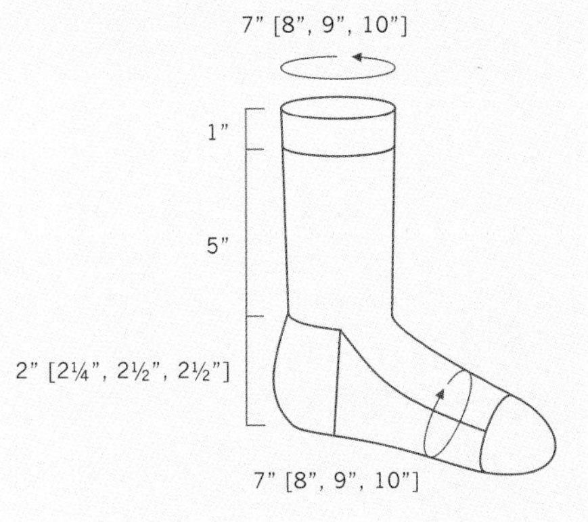

4 TURN HEEL

Continue working back and forth. Use short rows to turn heel as follows:

Row 1 (right side) Slip 1 purlwise with yarn in back, k16 [18, 20, 22], ssk, k1, turn.

Row 2 (wrong side) Slip 1 purlwise with yarn in front, p7, p2tog, p1, turn.

Row 3 Slip 1 purlwise with yarn in back, knit to one stitch before gap caused by turn on previous row, ssk (using one stitch from each side of gap), k1, turn.

Row 4 Slip 1 purlwise with yarn in front, purl to one stitch before gap caused by turn on previous row, p2tog (using one stitch from each side of gap), p1, turn.

Repeat last 2 rows until all heel stitches have been worked, ending ready to work a right side row. 18 [20, 22, 24] heel stitches.

5 FOOT

Resume working in the round as follows: Slip 1 purlwise with yarn in back, k8 [9, 10, 11]. Mark beginning of round. Knit remaining heel stitches, pick up and knit into each slipped stitch along edge of heel flap, make 1, mark right side of foot, work chart C across held stitches, mark left side of foot, make 1, pick up and knit into each slipped stitch along edge of heel flap, knit to end of round.

Right and left side markers divide foot into top of foot section (previously held stitches) and sole. Decrease 2 sole stitches every other round as follows:

Round 1 Knit to 2 stitches before right side of foot, k2tog, work chart C to left side of foot, ssk, knit to end of round. 2 stitches decreased.

Round 2 Knit to right side of foot, work chart C to left side of foot, knit to end of round.

Repeat last 2 rounds until 62 [72, 80, 90] stitches remain—34 [40, 44, 50] top of foot stitches and 28 [32, 36, 40] sole stitches.

Continue working even, without decreasing sole stitches, until foot measures 2 inches less than desired length from back of heel turn, ending with row 5 of chart C.

6 SET UP FOR TOE

Decrease 6 [8, 8, 10] stitches as follows: Knit to right side of foot, work chart D (repeating marked section 3 [4, 4, 5] times), knit to end of round. 56 [64, 72, 80] stitches remain.

7 TOE

Knit to right side of foot. This is the new beginning of round.

Round 1 Knit to end of round.

Round 2 K1, ssk, knit to 3 stitches before left side of foot, k2tog, k2 (one stitch before and one stitch after left side of foot marker), ssk, knit to 3 stitches before right side of foot, k2tog, k1. 4 stitches decreased.

Repeat last 2 rounds until foot measures desired length, ending after a decrease round. Graft top of foot stitches to sole stitches using Kitchener stitch (page 167). Weave in ends and block.

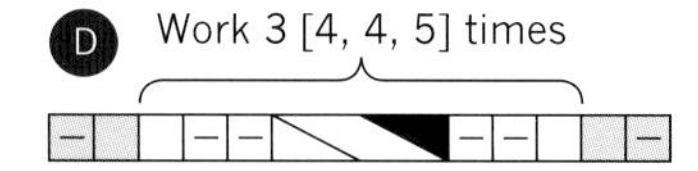

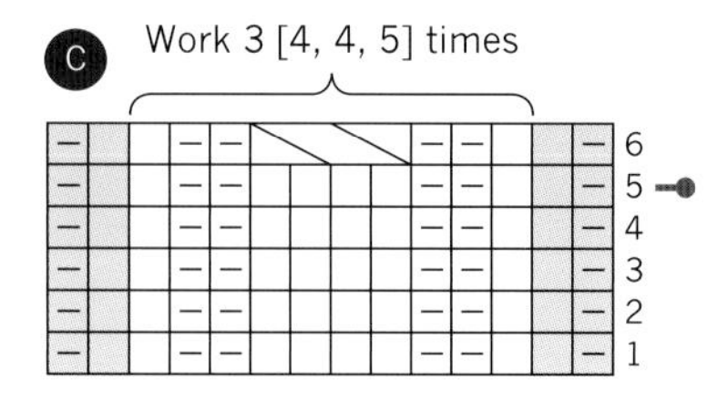

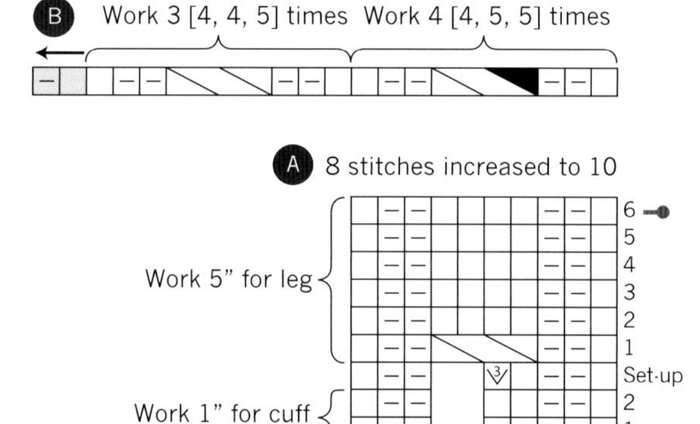

Knit

Purl

Knit into front, back, front of same stitch

Slip 2 to cable needle and hold in front, knit 2 from left needle, knit 2 from cable needle.

Slip 2 to cable needle and hold in front. Knit 1 stitch from cable needle together with 1 stitch from left needle—twice. 2 stitches decreased.

End after this row and proceed to next section.

Size XS and M only—Other sizes ignore these squares.

Size XS and M only—Work 2 more stitches from the beginning of the next round to center pattern on top of foot.

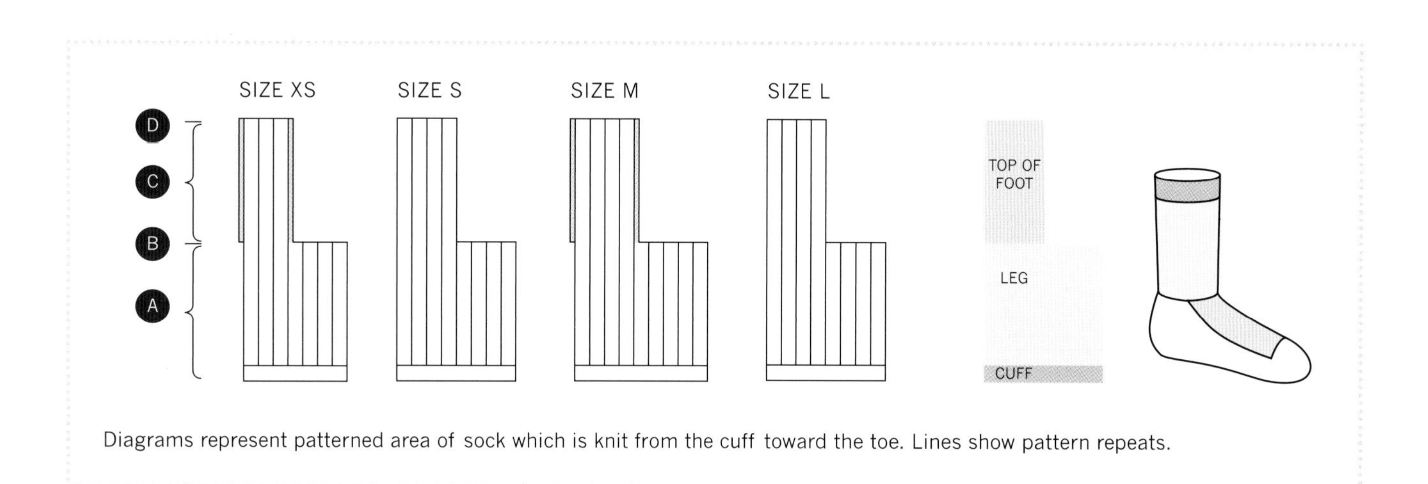

Diagrams represent patterned area of sock which is knit from the cuff toward the toe. Lines show pattern repeats.

Marilinda

Lines that flow in and out in a heart-shaped fashion create wide panels in this sock. Because each column is so wide, dividing for the heel flap and top of foot requires splitting the panels to center the pattern along the top of the foot. The patterning is continues down the heel of the sock. The small cable-like eyelets are created using a technique common in Japanese knitting.

1 LEG

Cast on 69 stitches and distribute such that each needle has a multiple of 23 stitches. Being careful not to twist, join for working in the round and mark beginning of round (page 168). Work chart A (page 32) by repeating first 2 rows for 1 inch for cuff, then work next 8 rows for set-up, increasing to 75 stitches. Work 2 vertical repeats of chart B, then rows 1 through 7 of chart B once more.

2 HEEL FLAP

K3, p2, k2tog, k1. 74 stitches.

Divide for heel flap by placing previous 37 stitches—7 stitches just worked and additional 30 stitches from end of previous round—on hold for top of foot. Heel flap is worked back and forth over next 37 stitches. Work back and forth over next 37 stitches following chart C (page 35). 34 heel stitches.

3 TURN HEEL

Continue working back and forth. Use short rows to turn heel as follows:

Row 1 (right side) Slip 1 purlwise with yarn in back, k18, ssk, k1, turn.

Row 2 (wrong side) Slip 1 purlwise with yarn in front, p5, p2tog, p1, turn.

Row 3 Slip 1 purlwise with yarn in back, knit to one stitch before gap caused by turn on previous row, ssk (using one stitch from each side of gap), k1, turn.

SIZES
One size

YARN
Cascade Heritage
75% superwash merino wool / 25% nylon
400 meters per 100g
1 skein of color #5614

NEEDLES
US Size 1 / 2.25mm
or size needed to obtain gauge

NOTIONS
Cable needle, tapestry needle

GAUGE
In stockinette
32 stitches and 48 rows = 4"

In pattern
38 stitches and 48 rows = 4"

MEASUREMENTS

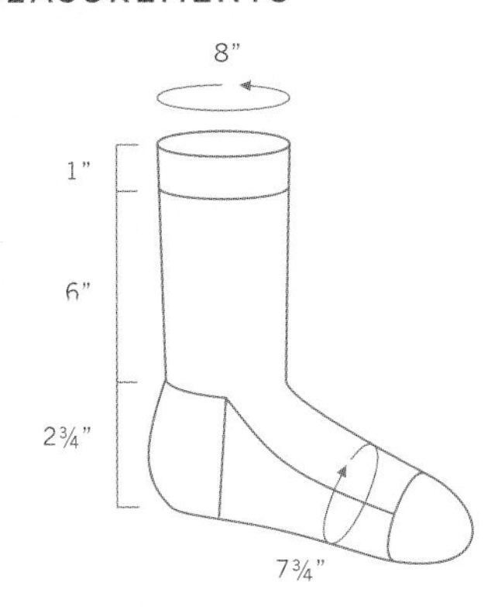

Row 4 Slip 1 purlwise with yarn in front, purl to one stitch before gap caused by turn on previous row, p2tog (using one stitch from each side of gap), p1, turn.

Repeat last 2 rows until all heel stitches have been worked, ending ready to work a right side row. 20 heel stitches.

4 FOOT

Resume working in the round as follows: Slip 1 purlwise with yarn in back, k9. Mark beginning of round. Knit remaining heel stitches, pick up and knit into each slipped stitch along edge of heel flap, make 1, knit first held stitch, mark right side of foot, ssk, p2, continue chart B (beginning on row 4) across next 25 held stitches, continue eyelet panel over next 3 stitches, p2, k1, mark left side of foot, knit last held stitch, make 1, pick up and knit into each slipped stitch along edge of heel flap, knit to end of round.

Right and left side markers divide foot into top of foot section (previously held stitches) and sole. 34 stitches remain on top of foot. Decrease 2 sole stitches every other round as follows:

Round 1 Knit to 2 stitches before right side of foot, k2tog, k1, p2, work in established pattern to 3 stitches before left side of foot, p2, k1, ssk, knit to end of round. 2 stitches decreased.

Round 2 Knit to right side of foot, k1, p2, work in established pattern to 3 stitches before left side of foot, p2, k1, knit to end of round.

Repeat last 2 rounds until 66 stitches remain—34 top of foot stitches and 32 sole stitches.

Continue working even, without decreasing sole stitches, until foot measures 2 inches less than desired length from back of heel turn, ending with row 1, 5, 9, 13, 17, 21, or 25 of chart B.

Decrease 2 stitches over next round by working in established pattern EXCEPT replace [chart symbol] with [chart symbol].

64 stitches remain—32 top of foot stitches and 32 sole stitches.

5 TOE

Knit to right side of foot. This is the new beginning of round.

Round 1 Knit to end of round.

Round 2 K1, ssk, knit to 3 stitches before left side of foot, k2tog, k2 (one stitch before and one stitch after left side of foot marker), ssk, knit to 3 stitches before right side of foot, k2tog, k1. 4 stitches decreased.

Repeat last 2 rounds until foot measures desired length, ending after a decrease round. Graft top of foot stitches to sole stitches using Kitchener stitch (page 167). Weave in ends and block.

Slip purlwise with yarn held to wrong side of work

Knit on right side / Purl on wrong side

Knit tbl on right side / Purl tbl on wrong side

Purl on right side / Knit on wrong side

Knit three times into one stitch by knitting into the front, back and front

Yarnover

Make 1

K2tog

Ssk

Slip 1 knitwise, knit 2 together, pass slipped stitch over

Pass third stitch on left needle over first 2 stitches and off needles, knit 1, yarnover, knit 1

Slip 1 purlwise, pass third stitch on left needle over first 2 stitches and off needles, pass slipped stitch on right needle back to left needle, k2tog, yarnover, ssk—2 stitches decreased

Pass third stitch on left needle over first 2 stitches and off needles, k2 —1 stitch decreased

Slip 2 to cable needle and hold to front, knit 2 from left needle, knit 2 from cable needle

Slip 2 to cable needle and hold to front, knit one stitch from cable needle together with stitch from left needle—twice. 2 stitches decreased

For leg only, end chart B immediately following row 7

Eyelet panel

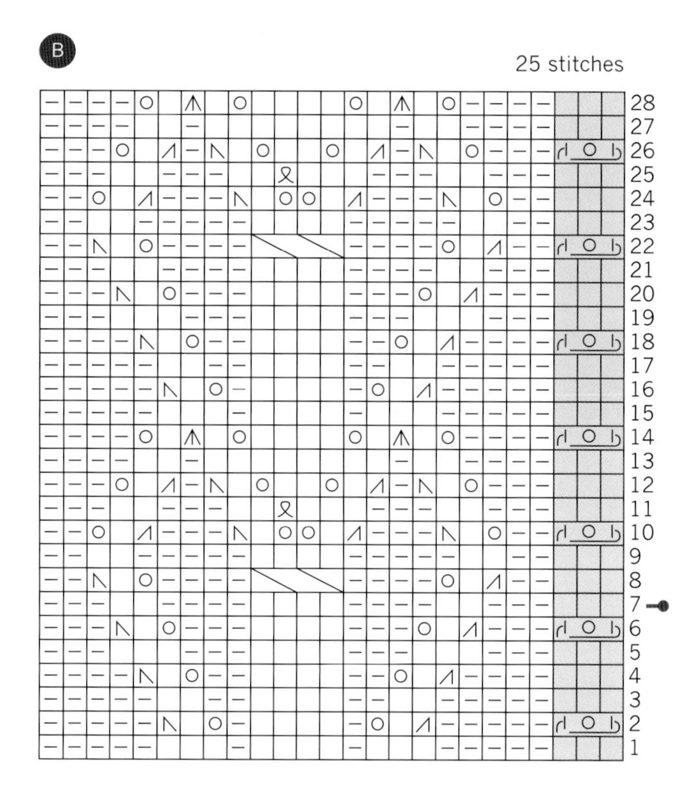

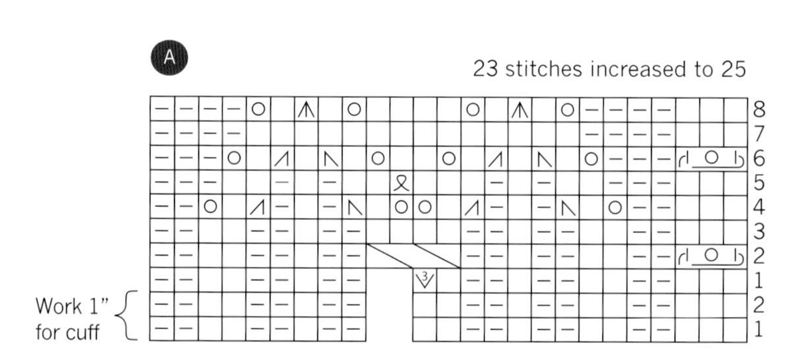

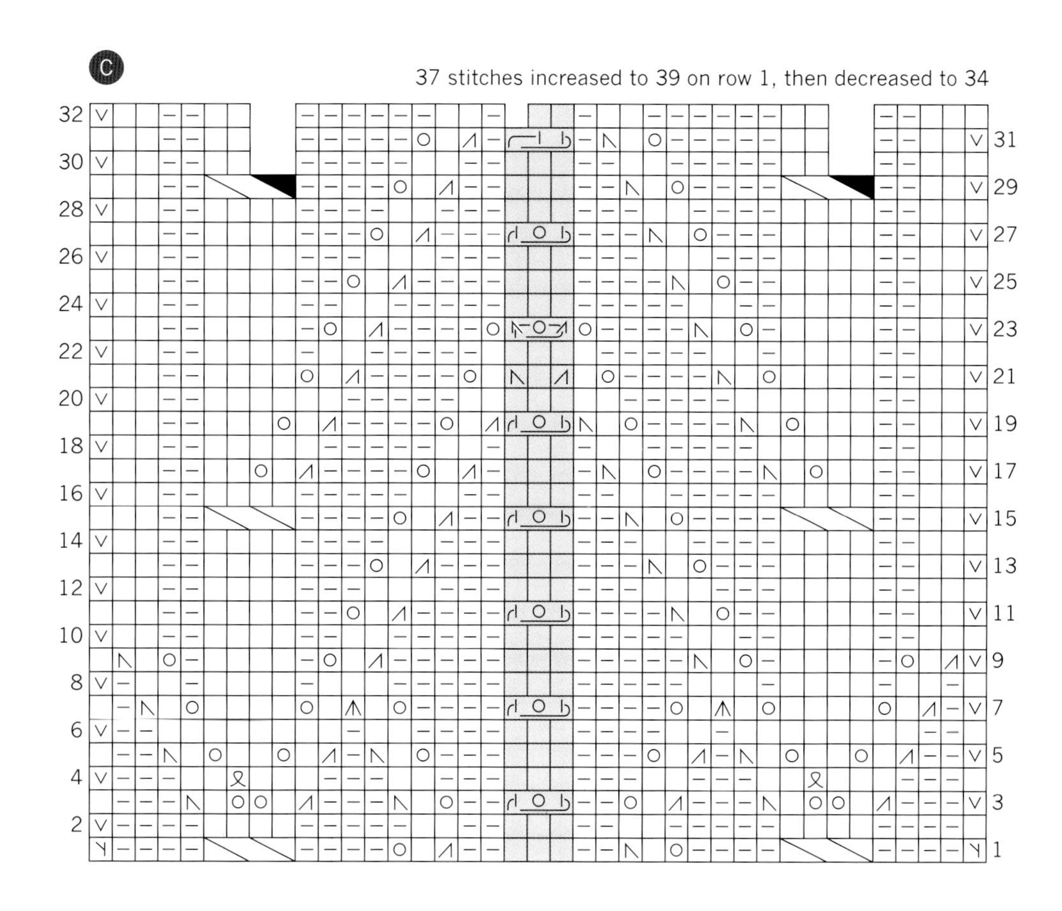

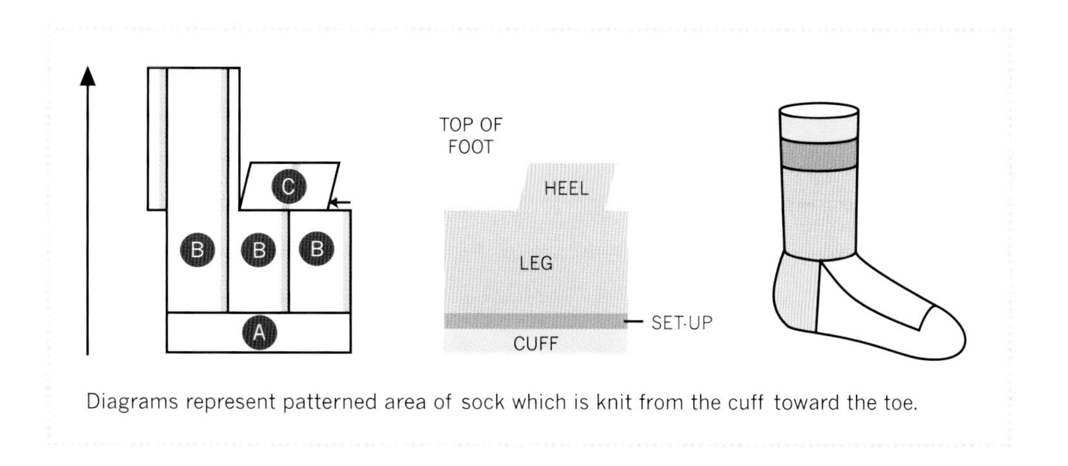

Diagrams represent patterned area of sock which is knit from the cuff toward the toe.

Stalagmite

These cabled socks are named after cave formations that slope upward from the ground. The four columns may appear distinct, but they are actually the same pattern staggered to begin at different places. Above the heel, an arm from one of the columns branches out and spreads into its neighbor's territory, creating the stalagmite shape and setting up for the heel flap.

0 NOTES

Left and right socks are mirror images of each other. Directions are the same for both unless otherwise indicated. The diagrams on page 42 outline the differences between the two socks. Charts C and D are located on pages 44 and 45 for left and right socks respectively. There are 4 versions of chart C, one for each size and side combination: Size S Left, Size L Left, Size S Right, and Size L Right. Make sure to use the appropriate chart for the size and side you are working.

1 LEG

Cast on 68 [80] stitches and distribute such that each needle has a multiple of 17 [20] stitches. Being careful not to twist, join for working in the round and mark beginning of round (page 168). Work charts A and B (page 43) according to diagram (page 42) by repeating first 2 rows for 1 inch for cuff, then working 13 set-up rows increasing to 84 [96] stitches, and then working two vertical repeats of 24-row repeat section.

2 SET-UP FOR HEEL FLAP

Work chart C (see Notes in Section 0) over next 42 [48] stitches, then continue in established pattern to end of round. Continue working from charts A, B and C through end of round 10. 80 [92] stitches.

SIZES
S [L] — shown in size S

YARN
Lorna's Laces Shepherd Sock
80% superwash wool / 20% nylon
215 meters per 2 oz
2 [3] skeins of Turquoise

NEEDLES
US Size 1.5 / 2.5mm
or size needed to obtain gauge

NOTIONS
Cable needle, tapestry needle

GAUGE
In stockinette
32 stitches and 48 rows = 4"

In pattern
42 stitches and 48 rows = 4"

MEASUREMENTS

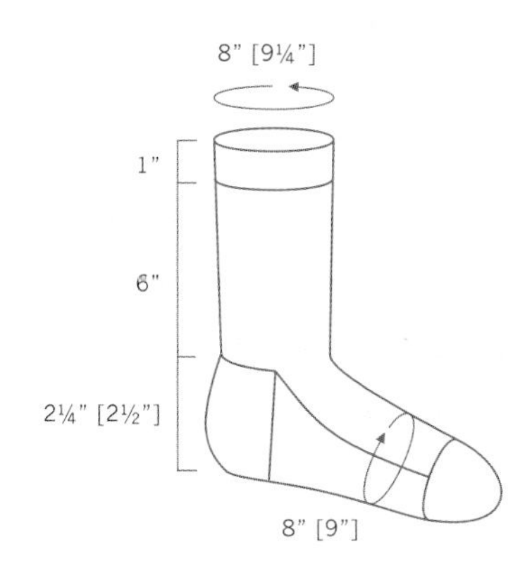

3 HEEL FLAP

Divide for heel flap by placing previous 41 [48] stitches on hold for top of foot. Heel flap is worked back and forth over remaining 38 [44] stitches from chart C plus 1 [0] additional stitch(es). Work back and forth following chart D (see Notes in Section 0) until heel flap measures 2¼ [2½] inches, ending ready to work a right side row. 35 [40] heel stitches.

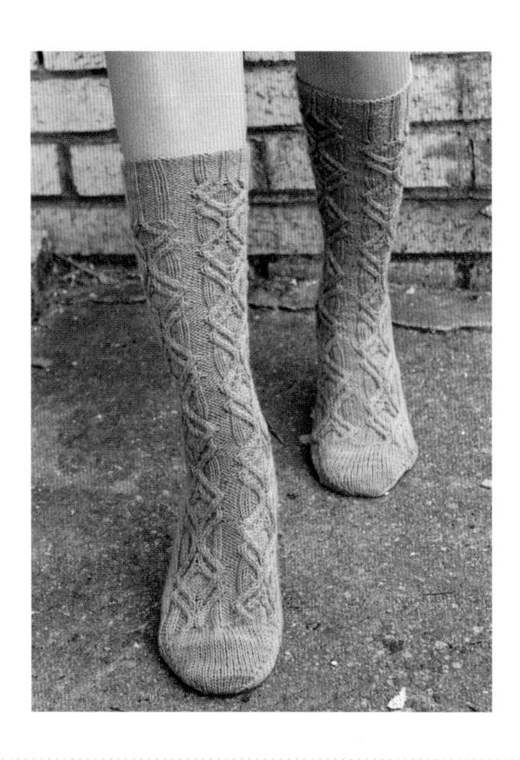

4 TURN HEEL

Continue working back and forth. Use short rows to turn heel as follows:

Row 1 (right side) Slip 1 purlwise with yarn in back, k19 [22], ssk, k1, turn.

Row 2 (wrong side) Slip 1 purlwise with yarn in front, p6 [7], p2tog, p1, turn.

Row 3 Slip 1 purlwise with yarn in back, knit to one stitch before gap caused by turn on previous row, ssk (using one stitch from each side of gap), k1, turn.

Row 4 Slip 1 purlwise with yarn in front, purl to one stitch before gap caused by turn on previous row, p2tog (using one stitch from each side of gap), p1, turn.

Repeat last 2 rows until all heel stitches have been worked, ending ready to work a right side row. 21 [24] heel stitches.

5 FOOT

Resume working in the round as follows: Slip 1 purlwise with yarn in back, k10 [11]. Mark beginning of round. Knit remaining heel stitches, pick up and knit into each slipped stitch along edge of heel flap, make 1, mark right side of foot, work held stitches in established pattern (note first stitch of chart is omitted for size S), mark left side of foot, make 1, pick up and knit into each slipped stitch along edge of heel flap, knit to end of round.

Right and left side markers divide foot into top of foot section (previously held stitches) and sole. Decrease 2 sole stitches every other round as follows:

Round 1 Knit to 2 stitches before right side of foot, k2tog, work in established pattern to left side of foot, ssk, knit to end of round. 2 stitches decreased.

Round 2 Knit to right side of foot, work in established pattern to left side of foot, knit to end of round.

Repeat last 2 rounds until 74 [84] stitches remain—41 [48] top of foot stitches and 33 [36] sole stitches.

Continue working even, without decreasing sole stitches, until foot measures 2 inches less than desired length from back of heel turn, ending with an even-numbered row other than 6 or 18 from charts A and B.

Decrease 8 stitches over next round by working in established pattern from charts A and B EXCEPT substitute first and last cables in both charts A and B (4 cables total) with cable decreases as follows:

Replace with .

Replace with .

Replace with .

Replace with .

66 [76] stitches remain—33 [40] top of foot stitches and 33 [36] sole stitches. For size L only, shift one stitch from each side of top of foot to sole so that stitches are divided evenly between top of foot and sole.

6 TOE

Knit to right side of foot. This is the new beginning of round.

Round 1 Knit to end of round.

Round 2 K1, ssk, knit to 3 stitches before left side of foot, k2tog, k2 (one stitch before and one stitch after left side of foot marker), ssk, knit to 3 stitches before right side of foot, k2tog, k1. 4 stitches decreased.

Repeat last 2 rounds until foot measures desired length, ending after a decrease round. Graft top of foot stitches to sole stitches using Kitchener stitch (page 167). Weave in ends and block.

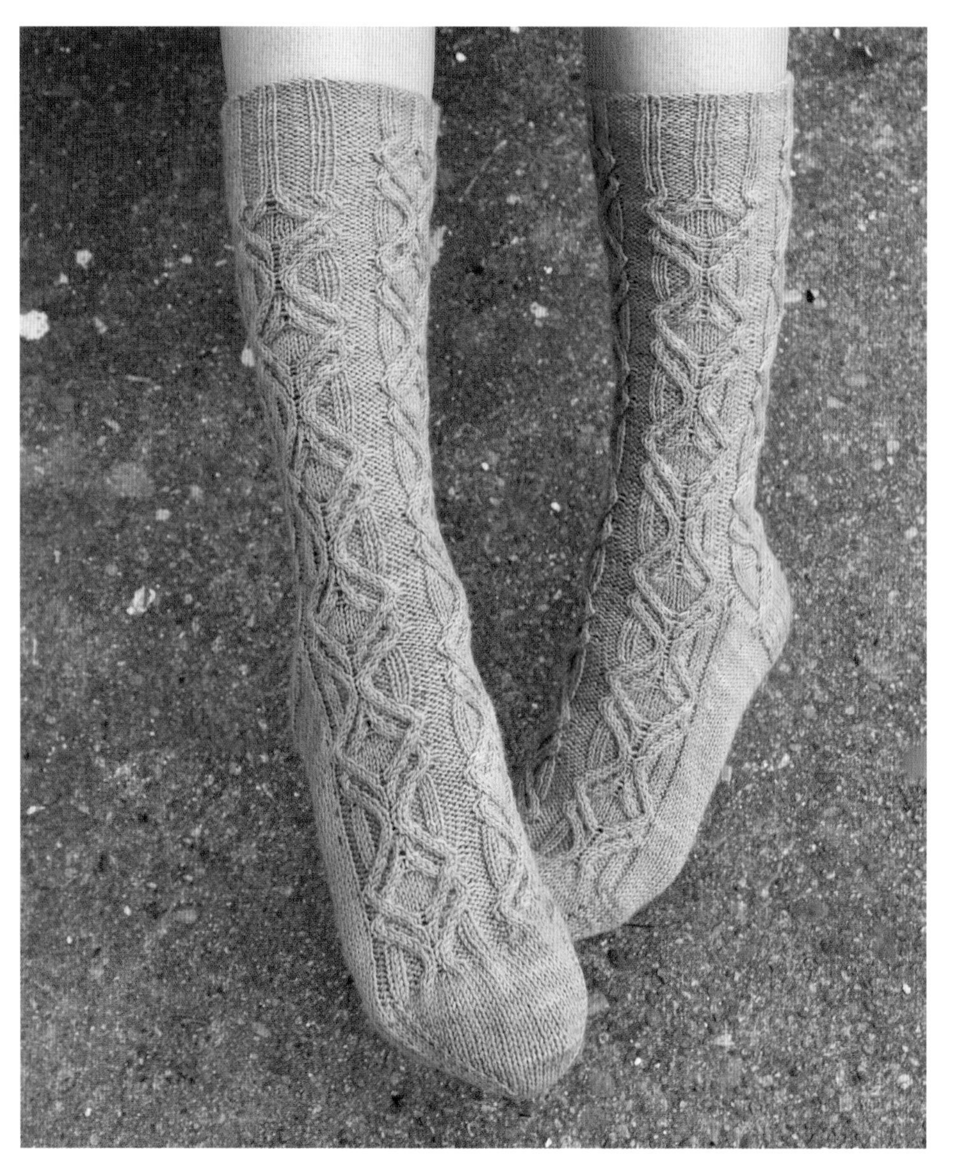

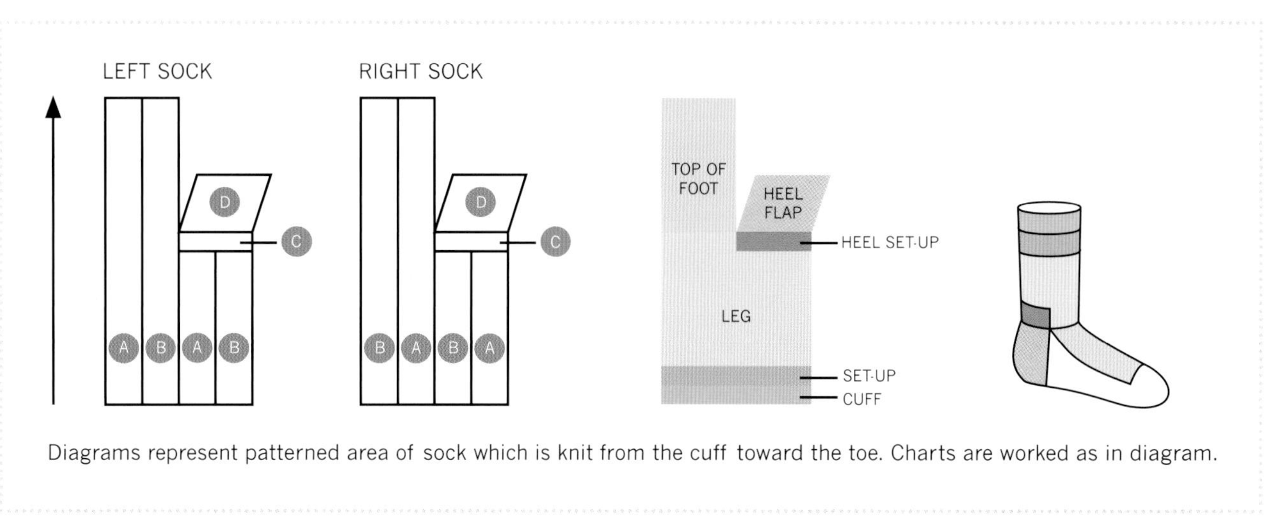

Diagrams represent patterned area of sock which is knit from the cuff toward the toe. Charts are worked as in diagram.

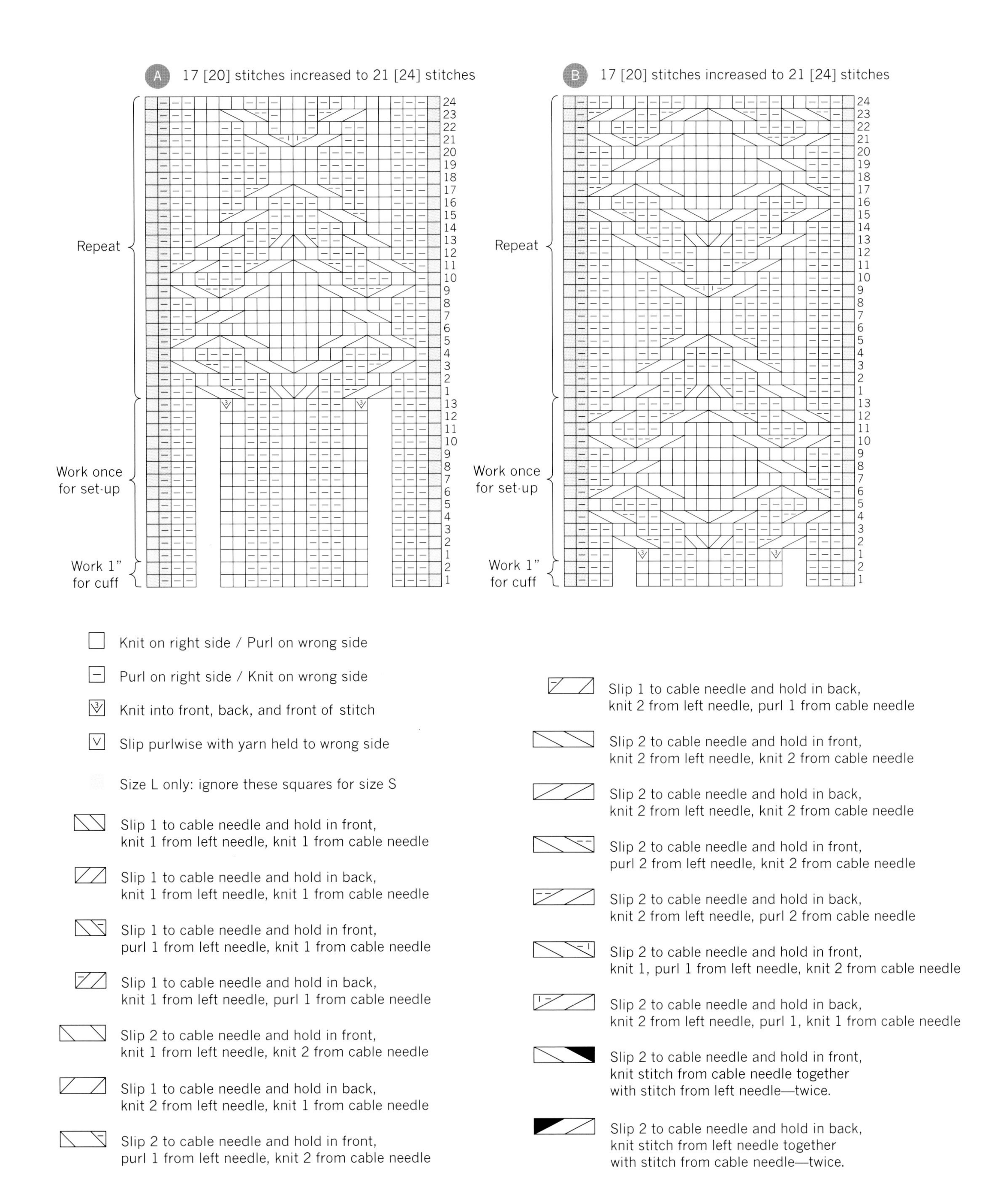
A
17 [20] stitches increased to 21 [24] stitches
B
17 [20] stitches increased to 21 [24] stitches
Repeat
Work once for set-up
Work 1" for cuff
Knit on right side / Purl on wrong side
Purl on right side / Knit on wrong side
Knit into front, back, and front of stitch
Slip purlwise with yarn held to wrong side
Size L only: ignore these squares for size S
Slip 1 to cable needle and hold in front, knit 1 from left needle, knit 1 from cable needle
Slip 1 to cable needle and hold in back, knit 1 from left needle, knit 1 from cable needle
Slip 1 to cable needle and hold in front, purl 1 from left needle, knit 1 from cable needle
Slip 1 to cable needle and hold in back, knit 1 from left needle, purl 1 from cable needle
Slip 2 to cable needle and hold in front, knit 1 from left needle, knit 2 from cable needle
Slip 1 to cable needle and hold in back, knit 2 from left needle, knit 1 from cable needle
Slip 2 to cable needle and hold in front, purl 1 from left needle, knit 2 from cable needle
Slip 1 to cable needle and hold in back, knit 2 from left needle, purl 1 from cable needle
Slip 2 to cable needle and hold in front, knit 2 from left needle, knit 2 from cable needle
Slip 2 to cable needle and hold in back, knit 2 from left needle, knit 2 from cable needle
Slip 2 to cable needle and hold in front, purl 2 from left needle, knit 2 from cable needle
Slip 2 to cable needle and hold in back, knit 2 from left needle, purl 2 from cable needle
Slip 2 to cable needle and hold in front, knit 1, purl 1 from left needle, knit 2 from cable needle
Slip 2 to cable needle and hold in back, knit 2 from left needle, purl 1, knit 1 from cable needle
Slip 2 to cable needle and hold in front, knit stitch from cable needle together with stitch from left needle—twice.
Slip 2 to cable needle and hold in back, knit stitch from left needle together with stitch from cable needle—twice.

D LEFT SOCK 39 [44] stitches decreased to 35 [40]

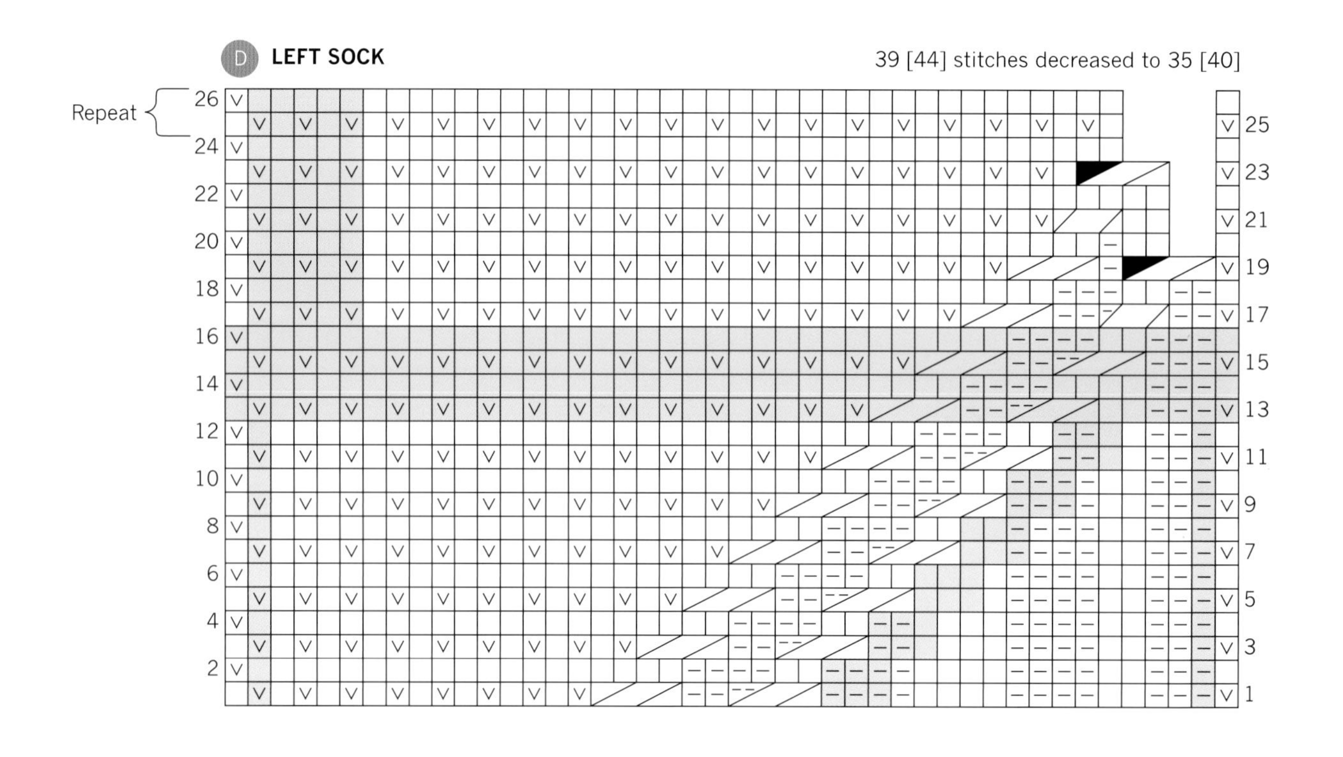

C LEFT SOCK SIZE S 42 stitches decreased to 38

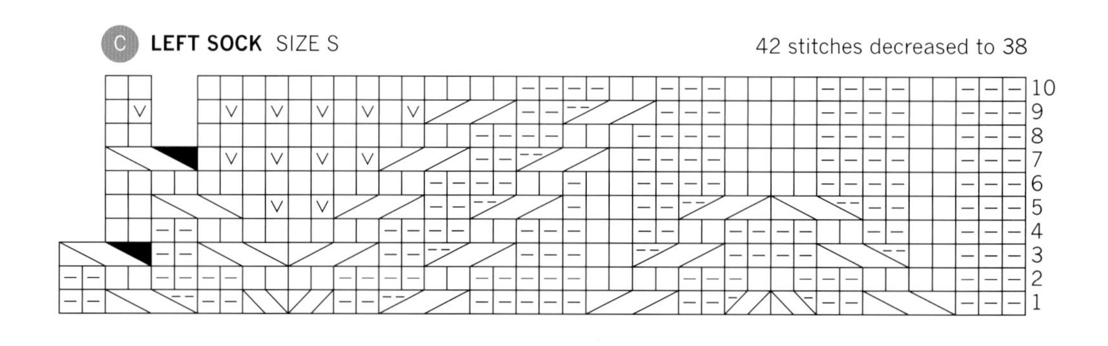

C LEFT SOCK SIZE L 48 stitches decreased to 44

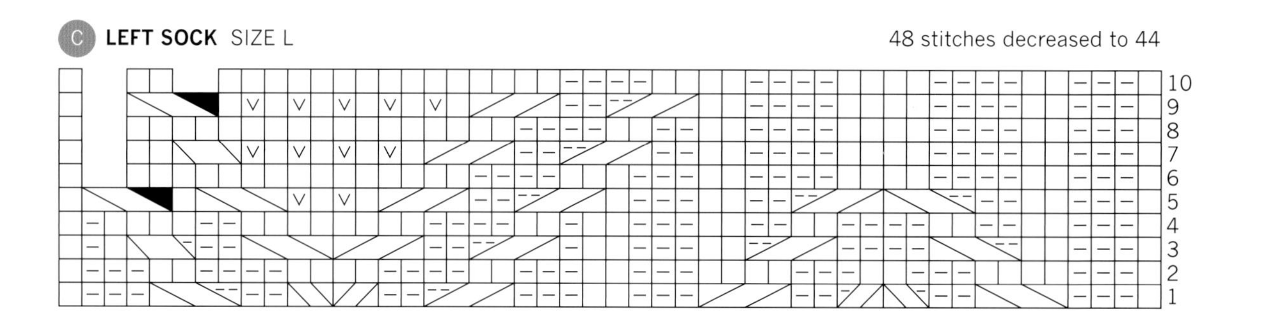

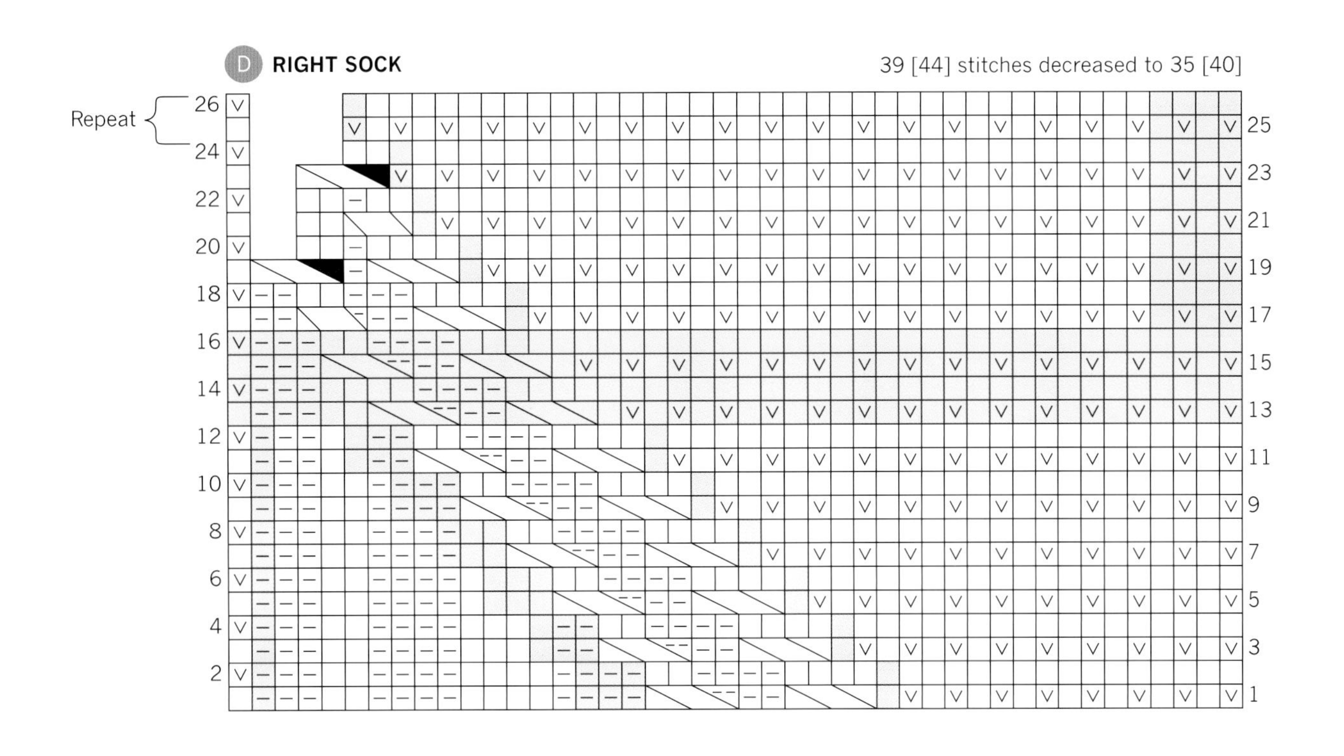
D RIGHT SOCK
39 [44] stitches decreased to 35 [40]
Repeat
26
24
22
20
18
16
14
12
10
8
6
4
2
25
23
21
19
17
15
13
11
9
7
5
3
1

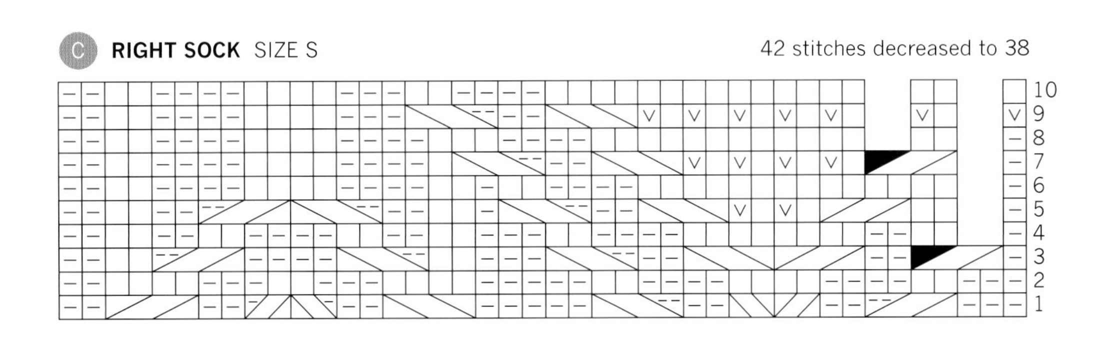
C RIGHT SOCK SIZE S
42 stitches decreased to 38
10
9
8
7
6
5
4
3
2
1

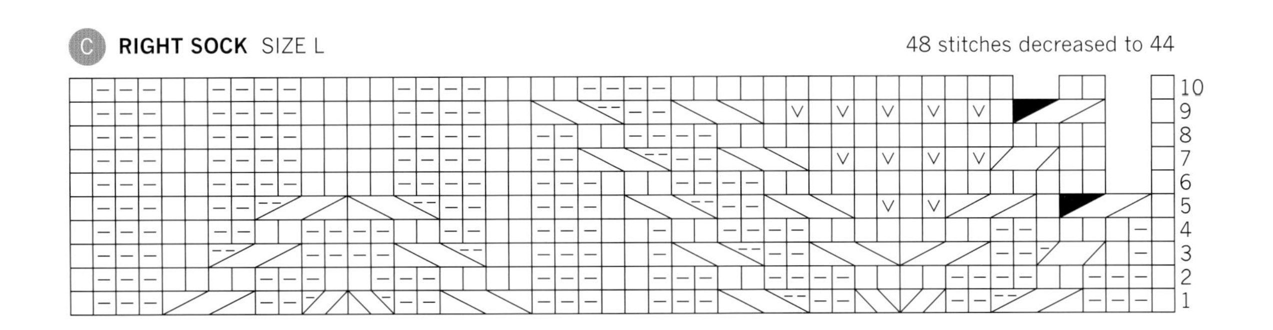
C RIGHT SOCK SIZE L
48 stitches decreased to 44
10
9
8
7
6
5
4
3
2
1

Lissajous

Lissajous curves are smooth, oscillating curves like the ones found in the panels on these socks. Four columns run vertically parallel to each other while colliding or avoiding obstacles along the way—a motif at the top front, another motif at the ankle, and calf shaping forces the columns to curve around them in the stocking version.

O NOTES

There are two versions for this pattern—knee high stockings with calf shaping and socks without calf shaping. The diagrams on page 55 outline the construction and differences between the two versions. Both versions use charts A, B, C, and D on page 56. The stocking version also uses charts E, F and G on page 57 for calf shaping.

Right and left socks/stockings are identical except chart G is mirrored for the stocking version. Use the appropriate chart G for the right or left stocking.

Directions for both versions are the same except where indicated. In particular, the Leg directions are broken out into separate sections, one for the stocking version on pages 51 and 52 and another for the sock version on page 52. Due to the extensive sizing of this pattern, numbers have been separated out into tables. Determine the numbers for your size using the tables on pages 48 and 49 before beginning.

SIZE AND MEASUREMENTS

Both versions There are 4 foot sizes, **F1** to **F4**, that correspond to the following ankle and foot circumferences. Select foot size by factoring in up to one inch of negative ease. For example, for a foot measuring 8½ inches, select size **F1**.

Foot Size		
	F1	7½"
	F2	8½"
	F3	9½"
	F4	10½"

SIZES
32 size combinations

Stockings shown are Foot Size F2 and Shaping Size S3. Socks shown are Foot Size F2 with no shaping.

YARN
Version 1 (stockings)
Louet Gems Fingering
100% superwash merino wool
185 yards per 50g
3-5 skeins of Cloud Grey
(size shown uses 3 skeins)

Version 2 (socks)
Shelridge Farm Soft Touch Ultra
100% wool
185 yards per 50g
2-3 skeins of Clover Flower
(size shown uses 2 skeins)

NEEDLES
US Size 1.5 / 2.5mm
or size needed to obtain gauge

NOTIONS
Cable needle, tapestry needle, stitch markers

GAUGE
In stockinette
32 stitches and 48 rows = 4"

In pattern
36 stitches and 48 rows = 4"

Stocking version only There are 8 shaping sizes, **S1** to **S8**. Measure the widest circumference around your calf and select Shaping Size using the following table, factoring in 2 to 3 inches of negative ease.

		Shaping Size							
		S1	**S2**	**S3**	**S4**	**S5**	**S6**	**S7**	**S8**
Foot Size	**F1**	10½"	11½"	12½"	13½"	14½"	15½"	16½"	17½"
	F2	11½"	12½"	13½"	14½"	15½"	16½"	17½"	18½"
	F3	12½"	13½"	14½"	15½"	16½"	17½"	18½"	19½"
	F4	13½"	14½"	15½"	16½"	17½"	18½"	19½"	20½"

TABLES

Determine the numbers for your size combination using these tables. **a** and **b** are determined by Foot and Shaping sizes using the first table. **c**, **d**, **e**, **f**, **g**, **h**, **i**, and **j** are determined by Foot size only using the second table. **k** is determined using Shaping Size only using the third table.

			Sock	Stockings · Shaping Size							
				S1	**S2**	**S3**	**S4**	**S5**	**S6**	**S7**	**S8**
Foot Size	**F1**	**a**	60	72	80	88	96	104	112	120	128
		b	72	84	92	100	108	116	124	132	140
	F2	**a**	68	80	88	96	104	112	120	128	136
		b	80	92	100	108	116	124	132	140	148
	F3	**a**	76	88	96	104	112	120	128	136	144
		b	88	100	108	116	124	132	140	148	156
	F4	**a**	84	96	104	112	120	128	136	144	152
		b	96	108	116	124	132	140	148	156	164

	Foot size			
	F1	**F2**	**F3**	**F4**
c	72	80	88	96
d	22	18	18	18
e	36	40	44	48
f	30	34	38	42
g	16	18	20	22
h	18	20	22	24
i	66	74	82	90
j	60	68	76	84

	Shaping Size							
	S1	**S2**	**S3**	**S4**	**S5**	**S6**	**S7**	**S8**
k	0	1	2	3	4	5	6	7

1 CUFF SET-UP

Cast on **a** stitches. Being careful not to twist, join for working in the round.

Establish pattern for sock Work chart A for front of leg, place marker, work chart A for back of leg. 12 stitches increased. **b** stitches.

Establish pattern for stocking Work chart A for front of leg, place marker, work halfway through chart A, place marker, work chart E, place marker, work chart F, place marker, work second half of chart A. 12 stitches increased. **b** stitches.

Both versions Continue in established pattern through row 8 of chart A.

2 CUFF AND CHART D

Begin working chart D as follows: Work chart D over front of leg, continue working chart A (and E and F for stocking version) over back of leg while placing markers before charts B and C within chart A.

Continue in established pattern through row 10 of chart D.

3 LEG - STOCKING VERSION ONLY

Introduce chart G as follows: Work chart D over front of leg, knit to marker, work chart B, knit to marker, work chart E, slip marker, work chart G, place marker, work chart F, knit to marker, work chart C, knit to end of round.

Continue in established pattern through end of chart D. On last row of chart D, place markers before charts B and C within chart D.

Work charts B, C, E, F and G as follows: Knit to marker, work chart B, knit to marker, work chart C, knit to marker (left side of leg), knit to next marker, work chart B, knit to marker, work chart E, work chart G, work chart F, knit to marker, work chart C, knit to end of round.

Continue in established pattern through end of chart G.

Next round Work in established pattern to one stitch before chart G marker, remove chart G marker and ssk, replace marker (now marking the center back of the leg), continue in established pattern to end of round **b** stitches.

Next round (Straight round) Knit to marker, work chart B, knit to marker, work chart C, knit to marker (left side of leg), knit to marker, work chart B, knit to marker, work stitches as set to marker (center back of leg), work stitches as set to marker, knit to marker, work chart C, knit to end of round.

Next round (Decrease round) Continue in established pattern to 2 stitches before center back of leg marker, k2tog, slip marker, ssk, continue in established pattern to end of round. 2 stitches decreased.

Repeat last 2 rounds until 1 stitch remains between center back of leg marker and next marker, ending after a Straight round.

Decrease 2 more stitches as follows: Knit to marker, work chart B, knit to marker, work chart C, knit to marker (left side of leg), knit to marker, work chart B, knit to 1 stitch before marker, remove next marker and k2tog, remove next 2 markers and ssk, knit to marker, work chart C, knit to end of round. **c** stitches.

Continue in established pattern without decreases until stocking measures approximately 4 inches less than desired leg length from back of knee to ground, ending with last row of charts B and C. Proceed to step 4.

3 LEG - SOCK VERSION ONLY

Continue working charts D, B and C as follows: Work chart D over front of leg, knit to marker, work chart B, knit to marker, work chart C, knit to end of round.

Continue in established pattern through end of chart D. On last row of chart D, place markers before charts B and C within chart D.

Work charts B and C over front and back of leg as follows: Knit to marker, work chart B, knit to marker, work chart C, knit to marker (left side of leg), knit to next marker, work chart B, knit to marker, work chart C, knit to end of round.

Continue in established pattern until sock measures approximately 5 inches from cast-on edge, ending with last row of charts B and C.

4 CHART D ON BACK OF LEG

Begin working chart D over back of leg as follows: Knit to marker, work chart B, knit to marker, work chart C, knit to marker (left side of leg), work chart D over back of leg.

Continue working charts B, C and D through row **d** of chart D.

5 HEEL FLAP

Divide for heel flap by placing next **e** stitches on hold for top of foot. Turn work so that wrong side is facing, and work chart D back and forth over remaining **e** stitches, except slip first stitch of each row purlwise with yarn held to wrong side of work. On last row of chart D, place markers before and after charts B and C within chart D.

Continue working back and forth for heel flap as follows.

Rows 1, 3 and 5 (wrong side) Slip 1 purlwise with yarn in front, purl to marker, work chart C, purl to marker, work chart B, purl to end of row, turn.

Rows 2 and 4 (right side) Slip 1 purlwise with yarn in back, knit to marker, work chart B, knit to marker, work chart C, knit to end of row.

Row 6 (right side) Slip 1 purlwise with yarn in back, knit to marker, remove marker, p1, k1 tbl, k2tog, p2tog, k1 tbl, k2tog, p1, remove marker, k10, remove marker, p1, k1 tbl, k2tog, p2tog, k1 tbl, k2tog, p1, remove marker, knit to end of row, turn. 6 stitches decreased.

Row 7 (wrong side) Slip 1 purlwise with yarn in front, purl to end, turn. **f** heel stitches.

6 TURN HEEL

Continue working back and forth. Use short rows to turn heel as follows:

Row 1 (right side) Slip 1 purlwise with yarn in back, knit **g**, ssk, k1, turn.

Row 2 (wrong side) Slip 1 purlwise with yarn in front, p5, p2tog, p1, turn.

Row 3 Slip 1 purlwise with yarn in back, knit to one stitch before gap caused by turn on previous row, ssk (using one stitch from each side of gap), k1, turn.

Row 4 Slip 1 purlwise with yarn in front, purl to one stitch before gap caused by turn on previous row, p2tog (using one stitch from each side of gap), p1, turn.

Repeat last 2 rows until all heel stitches have been worked, ending ready to work a right side row. **h** heel stitches.

7 FOOT

Resume working in the round as follows: Slip 1 purlwise with yarn in back, knit halfway across heel stitches and mark beginning of round. Knit remaining heel stitches, pick up and knit into each slipped stitch along edge of heel flap, make 1, mark right side of foot, work in established pattern across held stitches, mark left side of foot, make 1, pick up and knit into each slipped stitch along edge of heel flap, knit to end of round.

Right and left side markers divide foot into top of foot section (previously held stitches) and sole. Decrease 2 sole stitches every other round as follows:

Round 1 Knit to 2 stitches before right side of foot, k2tog, work established pattern to left side of foot, ssk, knit to end of round. 2 stitches decreased.

Round 2 Knit to right side of foot, work established pattern to left side of foot, knit to end of round.

Repeat last 2 rounds until **i** stitches remain—**e** top of foot stitches and **f** sole stitches.

Continue working even, without decreasing sole stitches, until foot measures 2 inches less than desired length from back of heel turn, ending on row 5, 6, 7 or 8 of charts B and C.

Decrease 6 stitches across top of foot as follows: Knit to marker, remove marker, p1, k1 tbl, k2tog, p2tog, k1 tbl, k2tog, p1, remove marker, k10, remove marker, p1, k1 tbl, k2tog, p2tog, k1 tbl, k2tog, p1, remove marker, knit to left side of foot, knit to end of round. **j** stitches.

8 TOE

Knit to right side of foot. This is the new beginning of round.

Round 1 Knit to end of round.

Round 2 K1, ssk, knit to 3 stitches before left side of foot, k2tog, k2 (one stitch before and one stitch after left side of foot marker), ssk, knit to 3 stitches before right side of foot, k2tog, k1. 4 stitches decreased.

Repeat last 2 rounds until foot measures desired length, ending after a decrease round. Graft top of foot stitches to sole stitches using Kitchener stitch (page 167). Weave in ends and block.

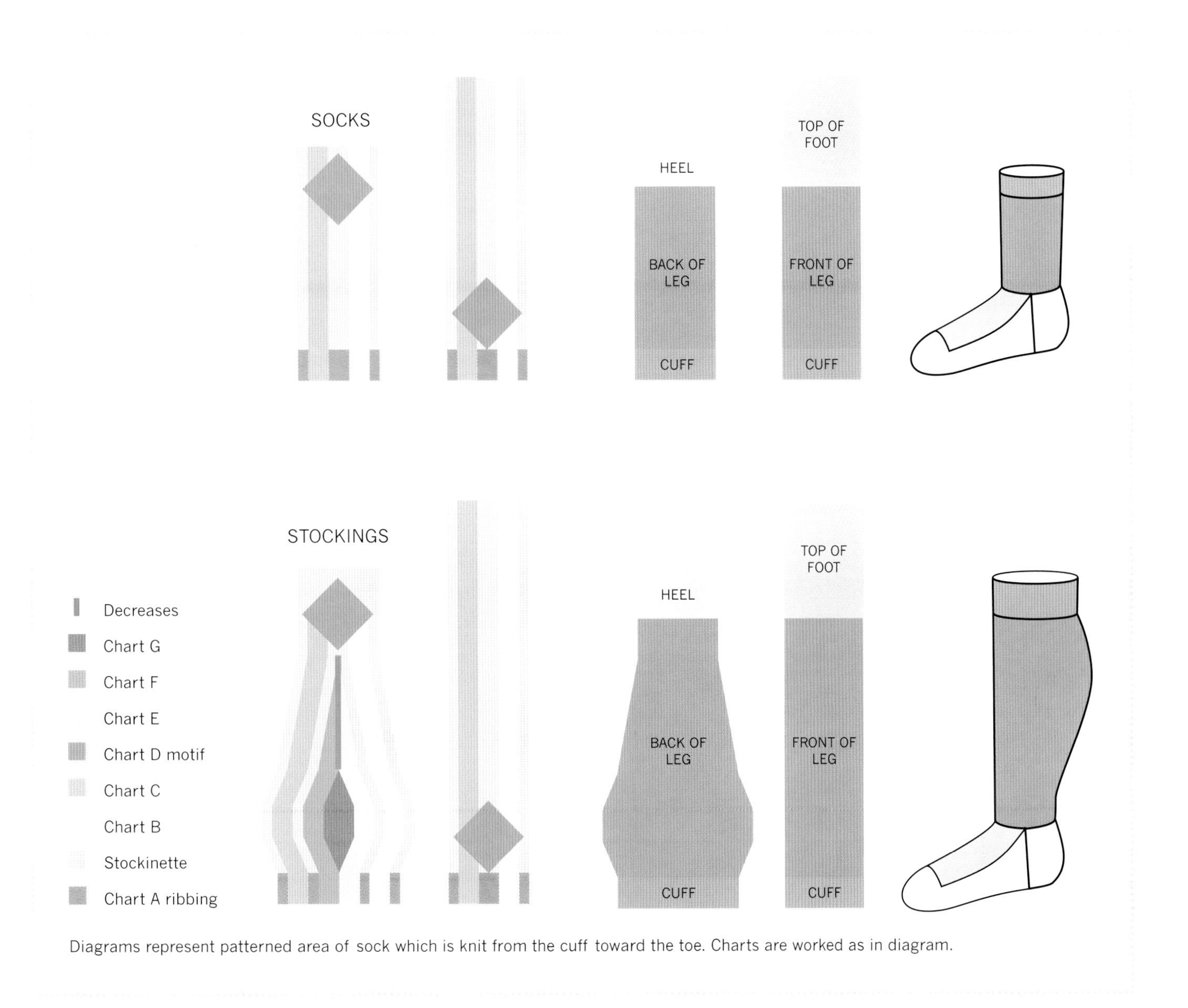

Diagrams represent patterned area of sock which is knit from the cuff toward the toe. Charts are worked as in diagram.

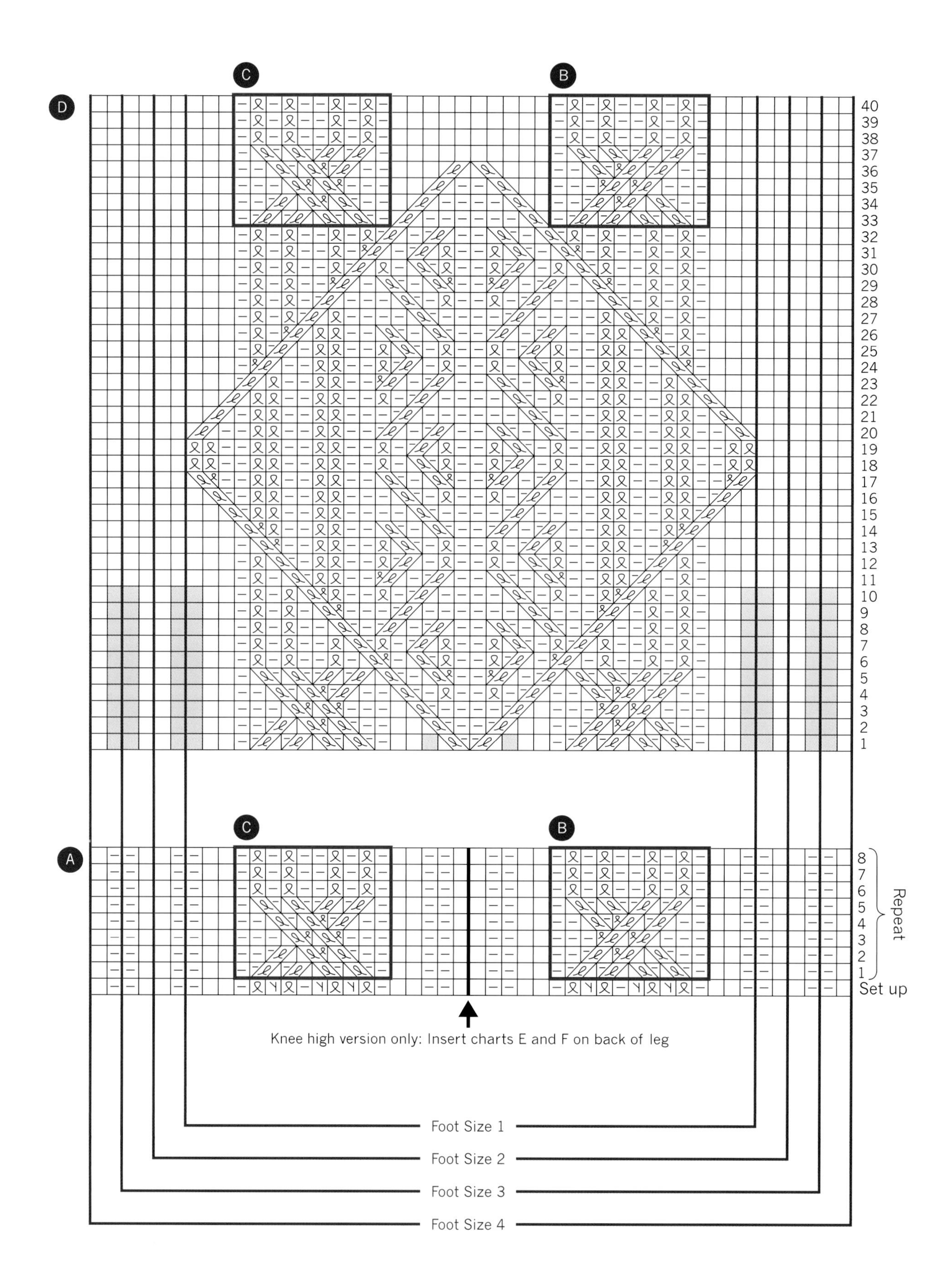
C
B
D
40
39
38
37
36
35
34
33
32
31
30
29
28
27
26
25
24
23
22
21
20
19
18
17
16
15
14
13
12
11
10
9
8
7
6
5
4
3
2
1
C
B
A
8
7
6
5
4
3
2
1
Repeat
Set up
Knee high version only: Insert charts E and F on back of leg
Foot Size 1
Foot Size 2
Foot Size 3
Foot Size 4

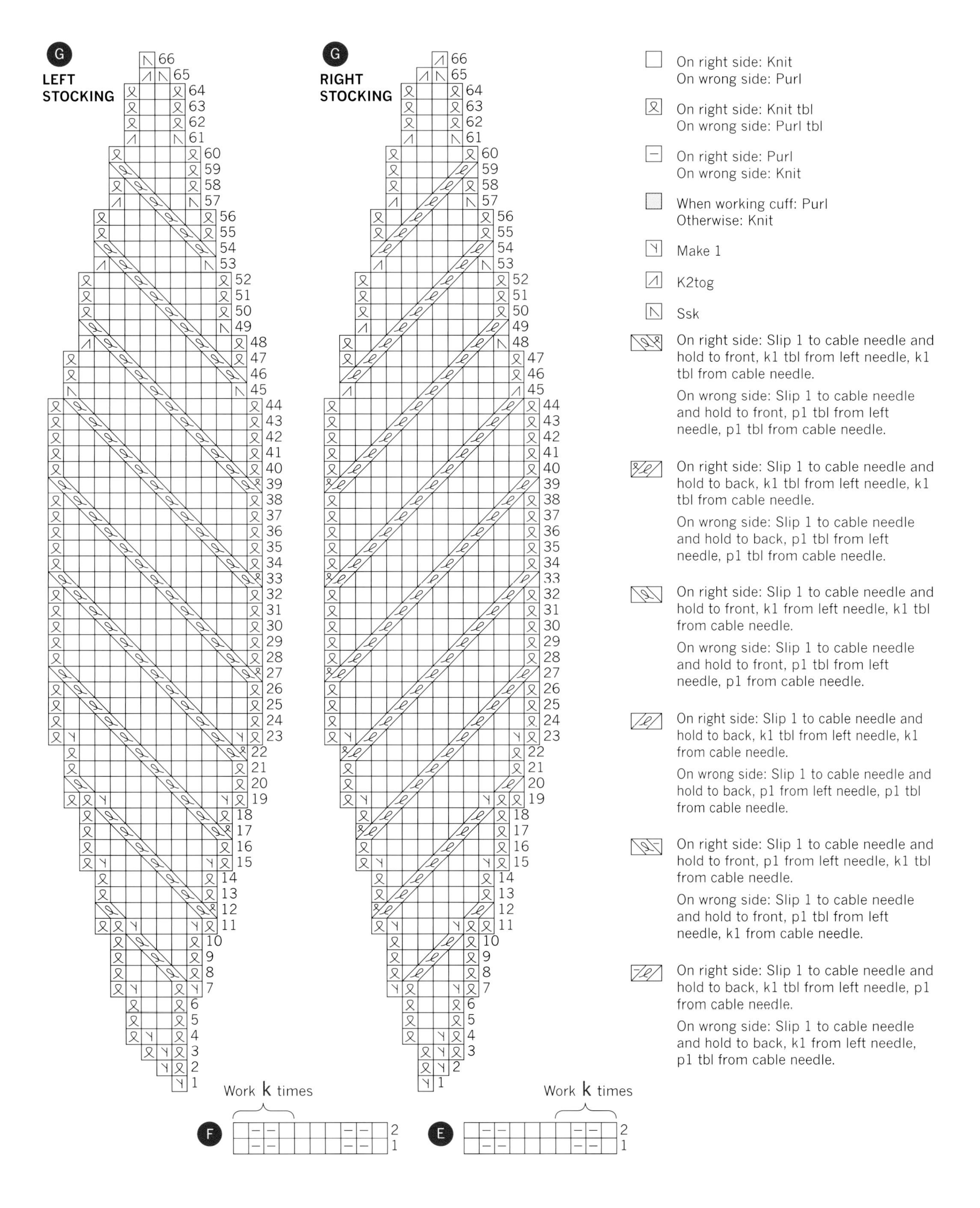
G
LEFT STOCKING
G
RIGHT STOCKING
On right side: Knit
On wrong side: Purl
On right side: Knit tbl
On wrong side: Purl tbl
On right side: Purl
On wrong side: Knit
When working cuff: Purl
Otherwise: Knit
Make 1
K2tog
Ssk
On right side: Slip 1 to cable needle and hold to front, k1 tbl from left needle, k1 tbl from cable needle.
On wrong side: Slip 1 to cable needle and hold to front, p1 tbl from left needle, p1 tbl from cable needle.
On right side: Slip 1 to cable needle and hold to back, k1 tbl from left needle, k1 tbl from cable needle.
On wrong side: Slip 1 to cable needle and hold to back, p1 tbl from left needle, p1 tbl from cable needle.
On right side: Slip 1 to cable needle and hold to front, k1 from left needle, k1 tbl from cable needle.
On wrong side: Slip 1 to cable needle and hold to front, p1 tbl from left needle, p1 from cable needle.
On right side: Slip 1 to cable needle and hold to back, k1 tbl from left needle, k1 from cable needle.
On wrong side: Slip 1 to cable needle and hold to back, p1 from left needle, p1 tbl from cable needle.
On right side: Slip 1 to cable needle and hold to front, p1 from left needle, k1 tbl from cable needle.
On wrong side: Slip 1 to cable needle and hold to front, p1 tbl from left needle, k1 from cable needle.
On right side: Slip 1 to cable needle and hold to back, k1 tbl from left needle, p1 from cable needle.
On wrong side: Slip 1 to cable needle and hold to back, k1 from left needle, p1 tbl from cable needle.
Work k times
F
Work k times
E

CHAPTER 2

TESSELLATIONS

A tessellation is an arrangement of shapes on a surface that leaves no gaps between them. They can be created by using a single shape repeatedly (Monkey) or several different shapes (Clandestine). Each building block can appear as a well-defined piece (Wedge), they can flow vertically into one another (Gothic

Monkey Monkey Rhombus Twisted Flower

Spire), or they can meld horizontally (Rhombus). A grid-like patterning is simplest (Monkey) while offset rows can be used to create a brick-like structure (Twisted Flower), or perhaps there aren't rows in the normal sense at all (Wedge). Despite the underlying geometry, these patterns can be quite organic.

Just like column-based patterns, tessellation-based patterns can seem complex, but both are made from smaller units that are repeated throughout. Once those smaller pieces are understood, the rest of the pattern will come naturally.

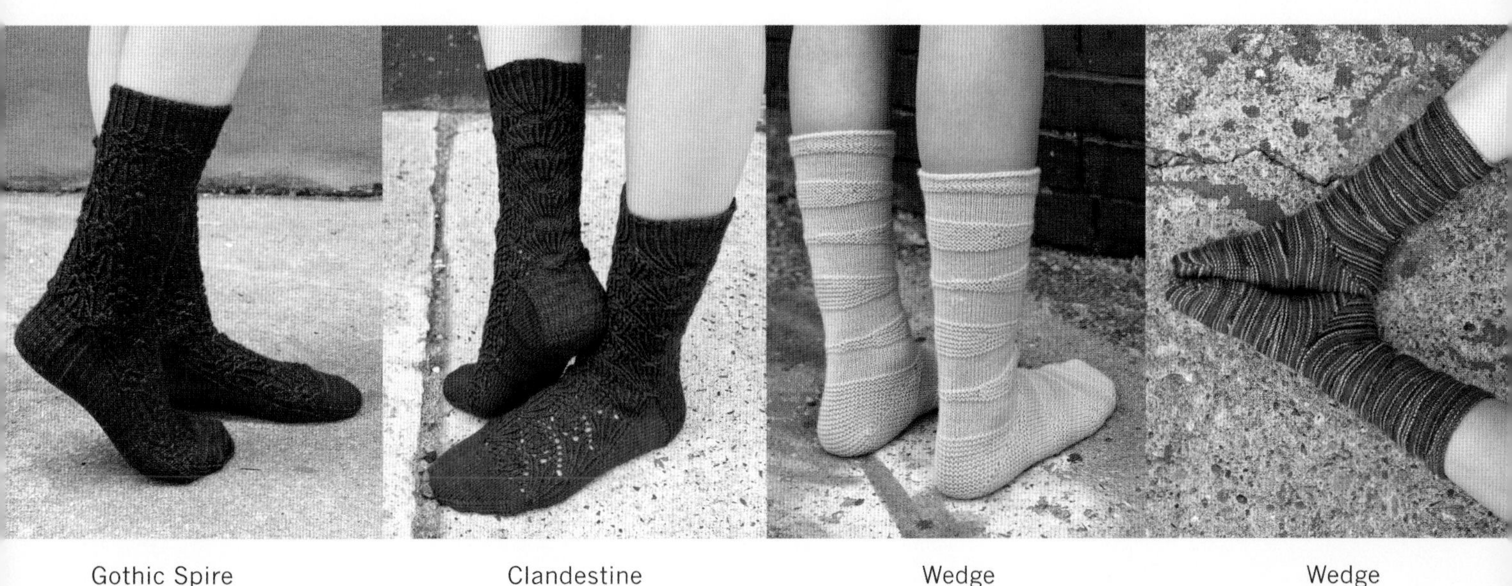

Gothic Spire | Clandestine | Wedge | Wedge

Monkey

This pattern is formed on a rectangular grid, perhaps the simplest tessellation. Each rectangular repeat forms a simple lace pattern that flows into the adjacent rectangles. Simple to memorize and great for showing off multi-colored yarn, the Monkey socks are a popular favorite and have been knitted by over ten thousand knitters across the globe. Embrace the sock-knitting monkey on your back.

1 LEG

Cast on 64 [80] stitches and distribute such that each needle has a multiple of 16 [20] stitches. Being careful not to twist, join for working in the round and mark beginning of round (page 168). Work chart S or L (page 65), depending on size, by repeating first 2 rows for 1 inch for cuff, then working 11 [13] row repeat section until piece measures approximately 6 inches from cast-on edge, ending after row 11 [13] of chart.

2 HEEL FLAP

Divide for heel flap by placing next 32 [40] stitches on hold for top of foot. Heel flap is worked back and forth over remaining 32 [40] stitches. Turn work so that wrong side is facing.

Row 1 (wrong side) Slip 1 purlwise with yarn in front, p31 [39], turn.

Row 2 (right side) Slip 1 purlwise with yarn in back, k31 [39], turn.

Repeat last 2 rows until heel flap measures 2¼ [2½] inches, ending ready to work a right side row.

3 TURN HEEL

Continue working back and forth. Use short rows to turn heel as follows:

Row 1 (right side) Slip 1 purlwise with yarn in back, k18 [22], ssk, k1, turn.

Row 2 (wrong side) Slip 1 purlwise with yarn in front, p7, p2tog, p1, turn.

Row 3 Slip 1 purlwise with yarn in back, knit to one stitch before gap caused by turn on previous row, ssk (using one stitch from each side of gap), k1, turn.

SIZES
S [L] — shown in size S (version 1) and L (version 2)

YARN
Version 1 Blue Moon Fiber Arts Socks That Rock Lightweight
100% superwash merino wool
360 yards per 4.5 oz
1 skein of Mustang Sally (Red)

Version 2 Pagewood Farm Chugiak
100% superwash merino wool
450 yards per 4 oz
1 skein of Leaf (Green)

NEEDLES
US Size 1 / 2.25mm
or size needed to obtain gauge

NOTIONS
Tapestry needle

GAUGE
In stockinette
32 stitches and 48 rows = 4"

In pattern
32 stitches and 48 rows = 4"

MEASUREMENTS

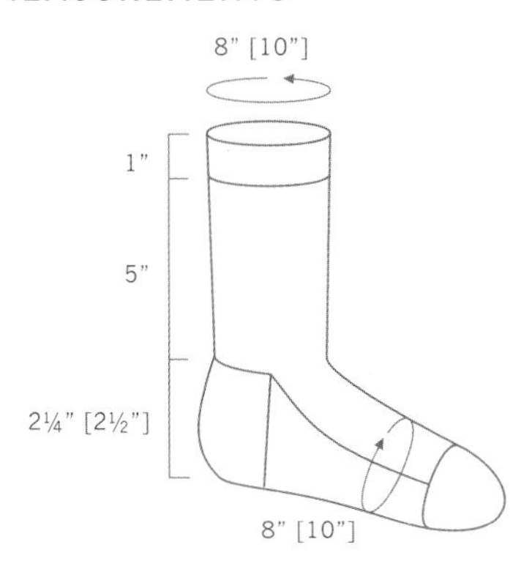

Row 4 Slip 1 purlwise with yarn in front, purl to one stitch before gap caused by turn on previous row, p2tog (using one stitch from each side of gap), p1, turn.

Repeat last 2 rows until all heel stitches have been worked, ending ready to work a right side row. 20 [24] heel stitches.

4 FOOT

Resume working in the round as follows: Slip 1 purlwise with yarn in back, k9 [11]. Mark beginning of round. Knit remaining heel stitches, pick up and knit into each slipped stitch along edge of heel flap, make 1, mark right side of foot, work held stitches in established pattern, mark left side of foot, make 1, pick up and knit into each slipped stitch along edge of heel flap, knit to end of round.

Right and left side markers divide foot into top of foot section (previously held stitches) and sole. Decrease 2 sole stitches every other round as follows:

Round 1 Knit to 2 stitches before right side of foot, k2tog, work in established pattern to left side of foot, ssk, knit to end of round. 2 stitches decreased.

Round 2 Knit to right side of foot, work in established pattern to left side of foot, knit to end of round.

Repeat last 2 rounds until 64 [80] stitches remain—32 [40] top of foot stitches and 32 [40] sole stitches.

Continue working even, without decreasing sole stitches, until foot measures 2 inches less than desired length from back of heel turn.

5 TOE

Knit to right side of foot. This is the new beginning of round.

Round 1 Knit to end of round.

Round 2 K1, ssk, knit to 3 stitches before left side of foot, k2tog, k2 (one stitch before and one stitch after left side of foot marker), ssk, knit to 3 stitches before right side of foot, k2tog, k1. 4 stitches decreased.

Repeat last 2 rounds until foot measures desired length, ending after a decrease round. Graft top of foot stitches to sole stitches using Kitchener stitch (page 167). Weave in ends and block.

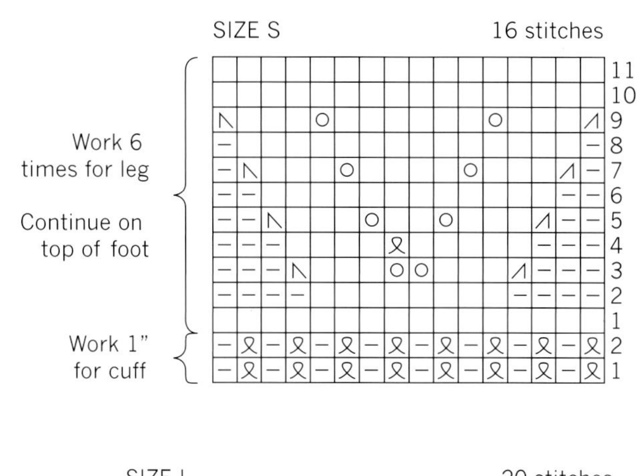

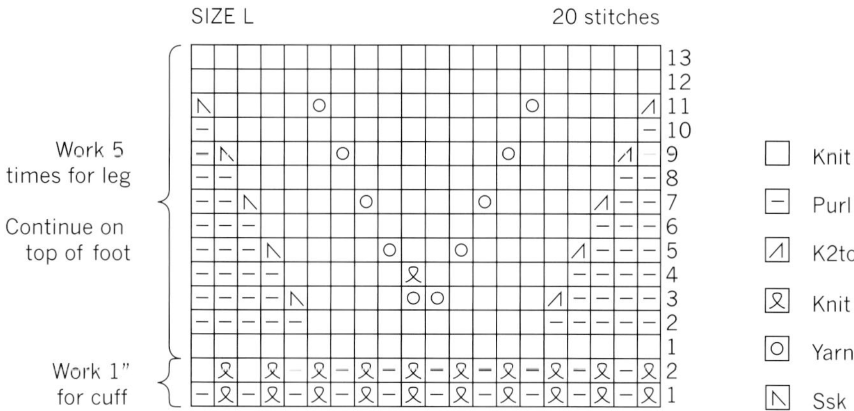

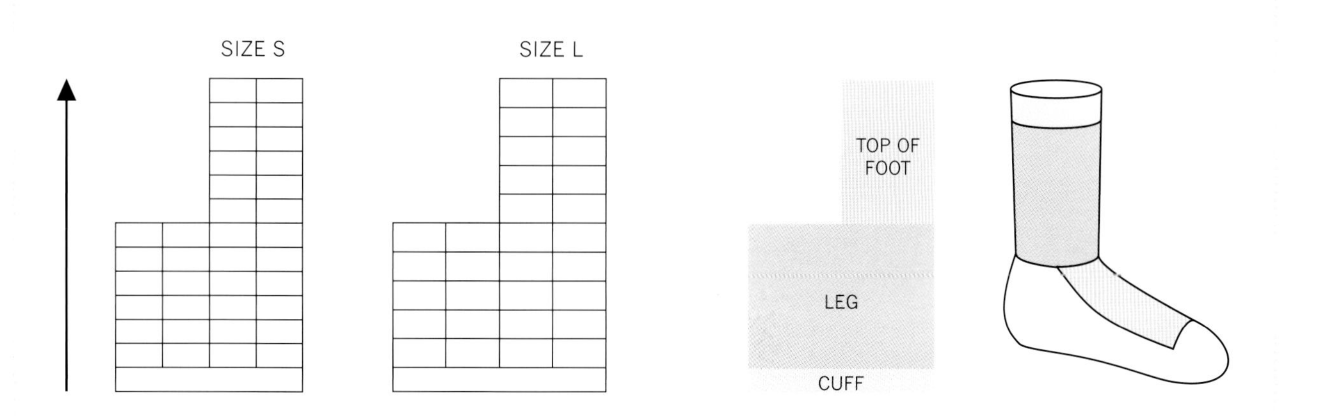

Diagrams represent patterned area of sock which is knit from the cuff toward the toe. Lines show pattern repeats.

Rhombus

Even though the charts for this pattern are rectangular, the concept is based on tessellating diamonds, also known in geometry as rhombuses. Cabled lines curve to form a lattice shape that is filled with a twisted rib texture, creating a floral shape. The ribbing flows from the cuff into the pattern and then into the heel flap while cable crosses alternate directions at the intersections.

1 CUFF

Cast on 60 [72] stitches and distribute such that each needle has a multiple of 12 stitches. Being careful not to twist, join for working in the round and mark beginning of round (page 168). Work chart A (page 70) by repeating first 2 rows for 1 inch for cuff, then working increase row. 70 [84] stitches.

2 LEG

Work chart B as indicated by diagram, ending after row 13 part way through the 3rd vertical repeat.

3 HEEL FLAP

Divide for heel flap by placing next 37 [44] stitches on hold for top of foot. Heel flap is worked back and forth over remaining 33 [40]. Turn work so that wrong side is facing.

Row 1 (wrong side) Slip 1 purlwise with yarn in front, work 32 [39] stitches as set (see Sidebar on page 68), turn.

Row 2 (right side) Slip 1 purlwise with yarn in back, work 31 [38] stitches as set, k1, turn.

Repeat last 2 rows until heel flap measures 2¼ [2½] inches, ending ready to work a right side row.

SIZES
S [L] — shown in size S

YARN
Cascade Heritage
75% superwash merino wool /
25% nylon
400 meters per 100g
1 skein of color #5602

NEEDLES
US Size 1 / 2.25mm
or size needed to obtain gauge

NOTIONS
Two cable needles, tapestry needle

GAUGE
In stockinette
32 stitches and 48 rows = 4"

In pattern
35 stitches and 48 rows = 4"

MEASUREMENTS

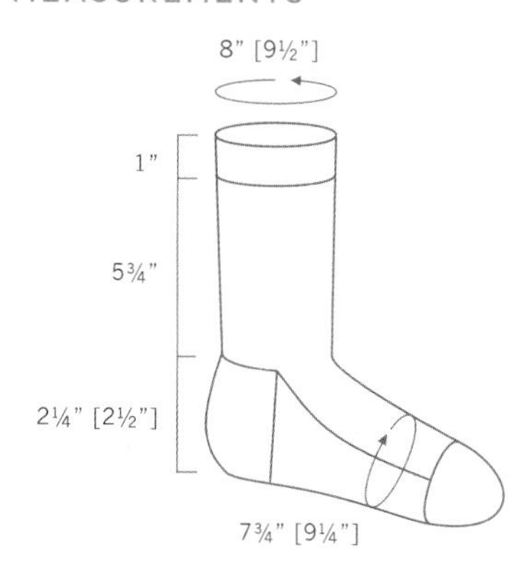

4 TURN HEEL

Continue working back and forth. Use short rows to turn heel as follows:

Row 1 (right side) Slip 1 purlwise with yarn in back, k17 [22], ssk, k1, turn.

Row 2 (wrong side) Slip 1 purlwise with yarn in front, p4 [7], p2tog, p1, turn.

Row 3 Slip 1 purlwise with yarn in back, knit to one stitch before gap caused by turn on previous row, ssk (using one stitch from each side of gap), k1, turn.

Row 4 Slip 1 purlwise with yarn in front, purl to one stitch before gap caused by turn on previous row, p2tog (using one stitch from each side of gap), p1, turn.

Repeat last 2 rows until all heel stitches have been worked, ending ready to work a right side row. 19 [24] heel stitches.

WORK STITCHES AS SET
While on the right side, purl the purls and knit all other stitches through the back loop.

While on the wrong side, knit the knits and purl all other stitches through the back loop.

5 FOOT

Resume working in the round as follows: Slip 1 purlwise with yarn in back, k9 [11]. Mark beginning of round. Knit remaining heel stitches, pick up and knit into each slipped stitch along edge of heel flap, make 1, mark right side of foot, work chart C (page 73) across held stitches, mark left side of foot, make 1, pick up and knit into each slipped stitch along edge of heel flap, knit to end of round.

Right and left side markers divide foot into top of foot section (previously held stitches) and sole. Decrease 2 sole stitches every other round as follows:

Round 1 Knit to 2 stitches before right side of foot, k2tog, work chart C to left side of foot, ssk, knit to end of round. 2 stitches decreased.

Round 2 Knit to right side of foot, work chart C to left side of foot, knit to end of round.

Repeat last 2 rounds until 66 [78] stitches remain—37 [44] top of foot stitches and 29 [34] sole stitches.

Continue working even, without decreasing sole stitches, until foot measures 2 inches less than desired length from back of heel turn, ending with an even-numbered row from chart C.

Decrease 4 [6] stitches over next round by working in established pattern from chart C except:

If working row 7 of chart C, substitute .

If working row 21 of chart C, substitute with , and for Size L only, substitute with .

If working any other row of chart C, omit the first 4 [6] increases: , , , .

62 [72] stitches remain—33 [38] top of foot stitches and 29 [34] stitches. Shift one stitch from each side of top of foot to sole so that there are 31 [36] stitches each.

6 TOE

Knit to right side of foot. This is the new beginning of round.

Round 1 Knit to end of round.

Round 2 K1, ssk, knit to 3 stitches before left side of foot, k2tog, k2 (one stitch before and one stitch after left side of foot marker), ssk, knit to 3 stitches before right side of foot, k2tog, k1. 4 stitches decreased.

Repeat last 2 rounds until foot measures desired length, ending after a decrease round. Graft top of foot stitches to sole stitches using Kitchener stitch (page 167). Weave in ends and block.

Slip 4 to cable needle and hold to back of work, knit 2 tbl from left needle, k2tog twice from cable needle. 2 stitches decreased.

Slip 2 to cable needle and hold to front of work, k2tog twice from left needle, knit 2 tbl from cable needle. 2 stitches decreased.

Knit tbl

Purl

K2tog

Ssk

Make 1 right

Make 1 left

Make 1 purl right

Make 1 purl left

Slip 1 to cable needle and hold to back, knit 1 tbl from left needle, knit 1 tbl from cable needle

Slip 1 to cable needle and hold to front, knit 1 tbl from left needle, knit 1 tbl from cable needle

Slip 4 to cable needle and hold to back, knit 2 tbl from left needle, slip 2 leftmost stitches on cable needle back to left needle and hold cable needle to front, purl 2 from left needle, knit 2 tbl from cable needle

Slip 2 to cable needle and hold to front, slip 2 to second cable needle and hold to back, knit 2 tbl from left needle, purl 2 from second cable needle, knit 2 tbl from first cable needle.

End chart B after row 13 and proceed to heel.

Shift beginning of the round 2 stitches to the right as follows: Work shaded squares as part of the pattern repeat, but omit them from the last pattern repeat, ending the round 2 stitches early.

Shift beginning of the round 2 stitches to the left as follows: Work shaded squares once and mark new beginning of round. Do not include shaded squares as part of the pattern repeat.

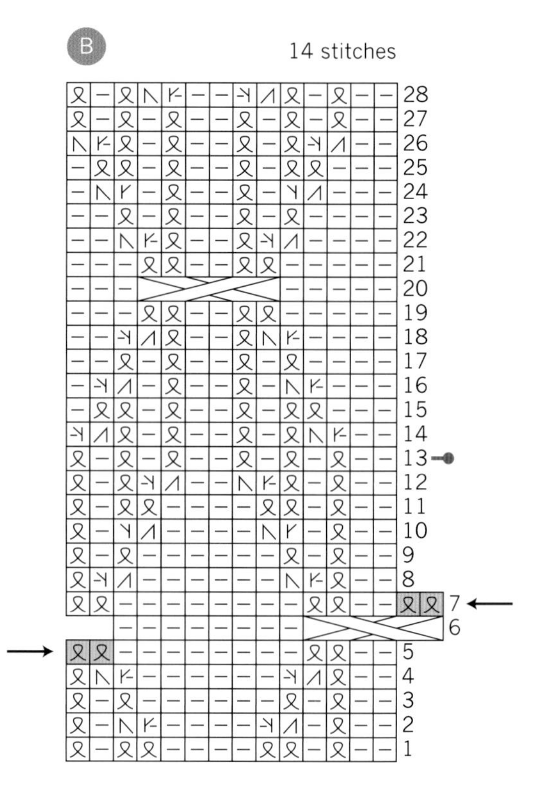

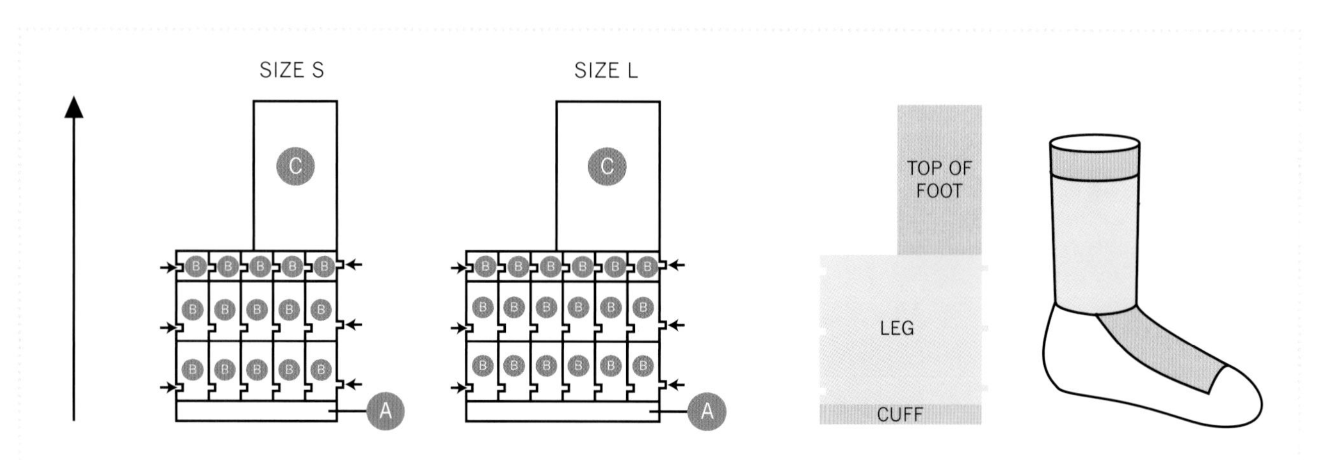

Diagrams represent patterned area of sock which is knit from the cuff toward the toe. Charts are worked as in diagram.

NO SMOKING

C

37 [44] stitches

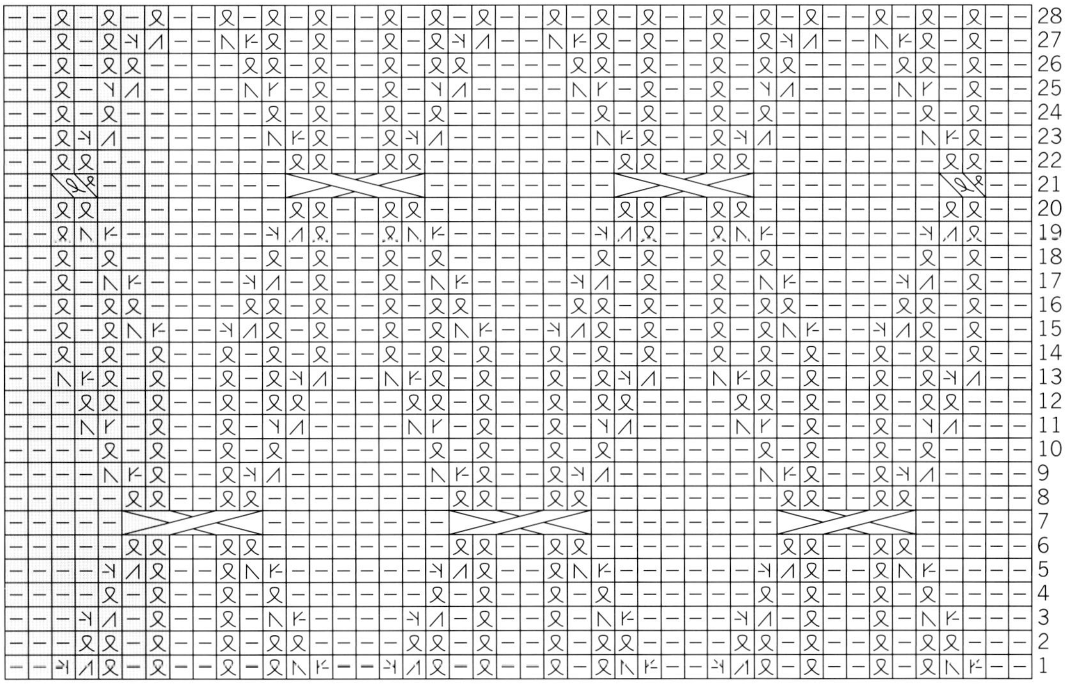

28
27
26
25
24
23
22
21
20
19
18
17
16
15
14
13
12
11
10
9
8
7
6
5
4
3
2
1

Size L only. Ignore these squares for size S.

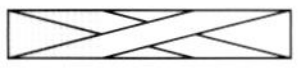

Size L, work same as if unshaded.

Size S, substitute:

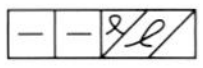

Twisted Flower

Twisted stitch cables combine with lacy eyelets to create the appearance of flowers and leaves in this adventurous pattern. The lacy leaves continue onto the heel flap making this sock beautiful from all angles. Despite the hard angles in the rectangular repeats, the cabled flowers are smooth and curved.

1 RIBBING

Cast on 72 stitches and distribute such that each needle has a multiple of 18 stitches. Being careful not to twist, join for working in the round and mark beginning of round (page 168). Work chart A (page 79) for one inch.

2 LEG

Work chart B. After completing chart B, shift beginning of round 9 stitches to left as indicated by chart. Work chart B once more. Do not shift beginning of round.

3 HEEL FLAP

Divide for heel flap by placing previous 38 stitches on hold for top of foot. Work back and forth for heel flap using chart C (page 78) over remaining 34 stitches, increasing to 36 heel stitches. Repeat rows 7 to 12 of chart C until heel flap measures approximately 2½ inches.

4 TURN HEEL

Continue working back and forth. Use short rows to turn heel as follows:

Row 1 (right side) Slip 1 purlwise with yarn in back, k20, ssk, k1, turn.

Row 2 (wrong side) Slip 1 purlwise with yarn in front, p7, p2tog, p1, turn.

Row 3 Slip 1 purlwise with yarn in back, knit to one stitch before gap caused by turn on previous row, ssk (using one stitch from each side of gap), k1, turn.

SIZES
One size

YARN
Cascade Heritage
75% superwash merino wool / 25% nylon
400 meters per 100g
1 skein of color #5617

NEEDLES
US Size 1 / 2.25mm
or size needed to obtain gauge

NOTIONS
Cable needle, tapestry needle

GAUGE
In stockinette
32 stitches and 48 rows = 4"

In pattern
36 stitches and 48 rows = 4"

MEASUREMENTS

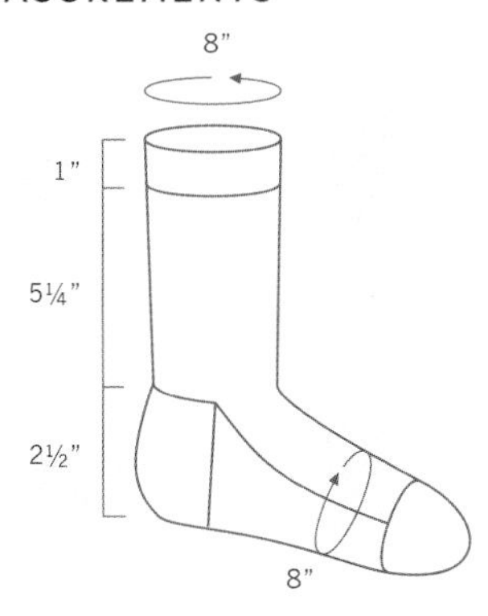

Row 4 Slip 1 purlwise with yarn in front, purl to one stitch before gap caused by turn on previous row, p2tog (using one stitch from each side of gap), p1, turn.

Repeat last 2 rows until all heel stitches have been worked, ending ready to work a right side row. 22 heel stitches.

5 FOOT

Resume working in the round as follows: Slip 1 purlwise with yarn in back, k10. Mark beginning of round. Knit remaining heel stitches, pick up and knit into each slipped stitch along edge of heel flap, make 1, mark right side of foot, work chart D across held stitches, mark left side of foot, make 1, pick up and knit into each slipped stitch along edge of heel flap, knit to end of round.

Right and left side markers divide foot into top of foot section (previously held stitches) and sole. Decrease 2 sole stitches every other round as follows:

Round 1 Knit to 2 stitches before right side of foot, k2tog, work chart D to left side of foot, ssk, knit to end of round. 2 stitches decreased.

Round 2 Knit to right side of foot, work chart D to left side of foot, knit to end of round.

Repeat last 2 rounds until 68 stitches remain—38 top of foot stitches and 30 sole stitches.

Continue working even, without decreasing sole stitches, until foot measures 2 inches less than desired length from back of heel turn. 64 stitches remain—34 top of foot stitches and 30 sole stitches.

6 TOE

Keeping pattern centered on top of foot, shift stitches as necessary between top of foot and sole so that each has 32 stitches.

Knit to right side of foot. This is the new beginning of round.

Round 1 Knit to end of round.

Round 2 K1, ssk, knit to 3 stitches before left side of foot, k2tog, k2 (one stitch before and one stitch after left side of foot marker), ssk, knit to 3 stitches before right side of foot, k2tog, k1. 4 stitches decreased.

Repeat last 2 rounds until foot measures desired length, ending after a decrease round. Graft top of foot stitches to sole stitches using Kitchener stitch (page 167). Weave in ends and block.

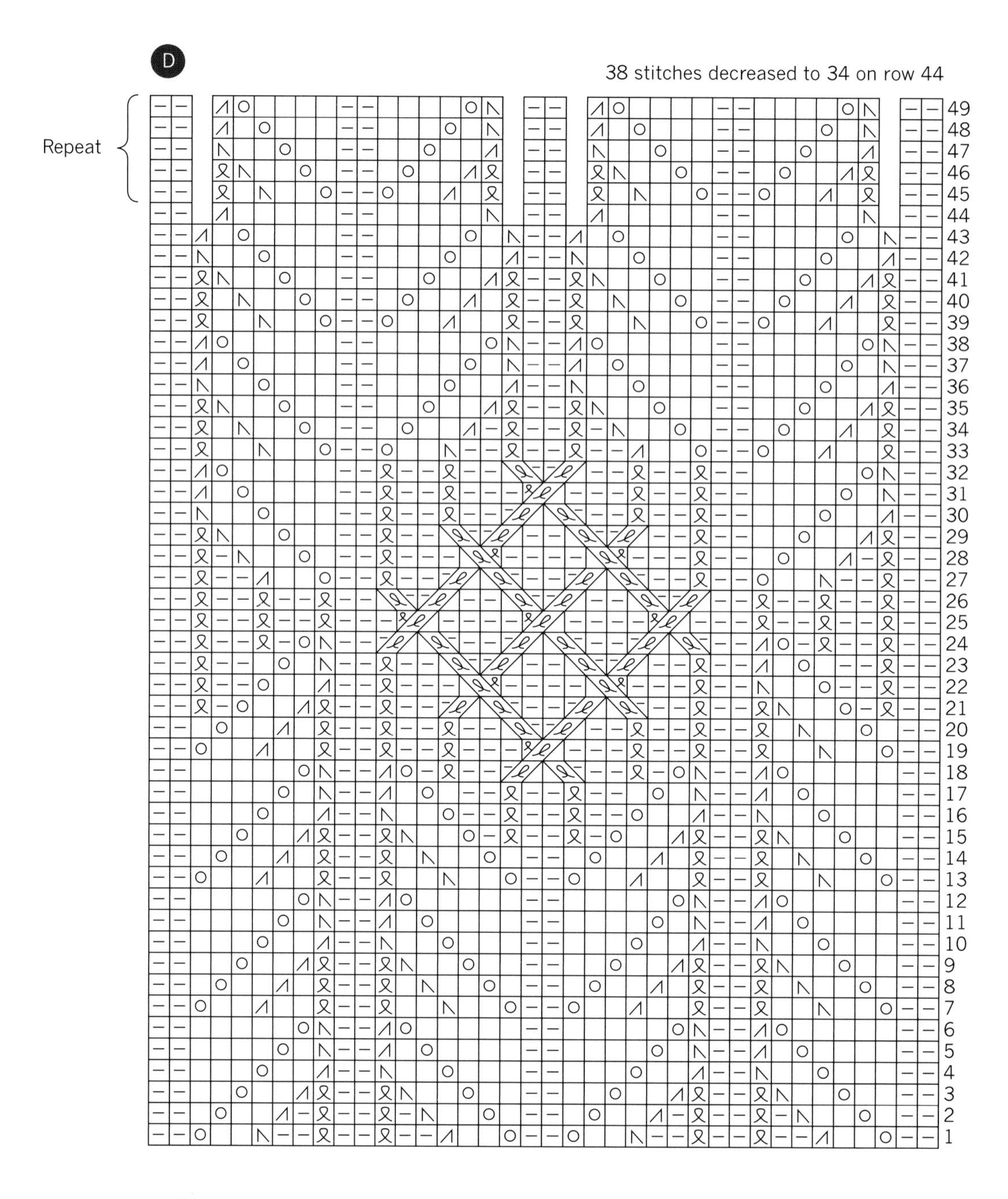
D
38 stitches decreased to 34 on row 44
Repeat
49
48
47
46
45
44
43
42
41
40
39
38
37
36
35
34
33
32
31
30
29
28
27
26
25
24
23
22
21
20
19
18
17
16
15
14
13
12
11
10
9
8
7
6
5
4
3
2
1

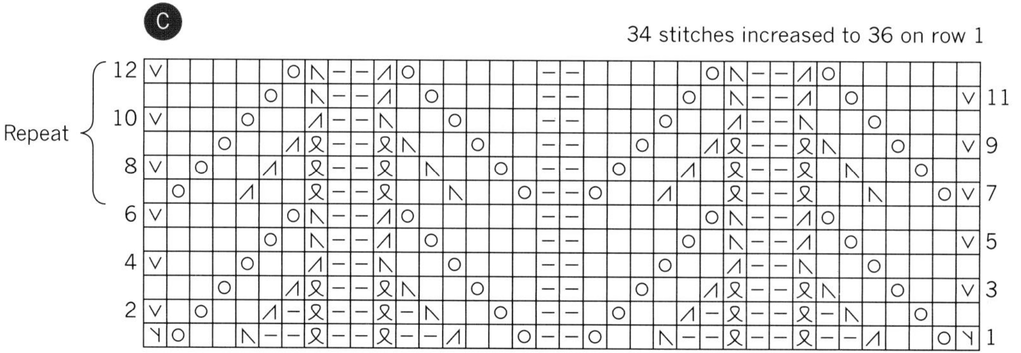
C
34 stitches increased to 36 on row 1
Repeat
12
11
10
9
8
7
6
5
4
3
2
1

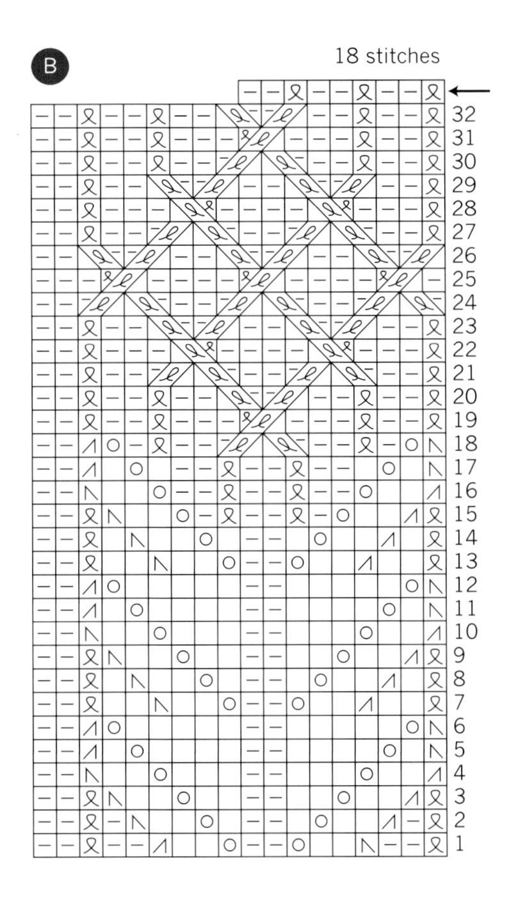

A

18 stitches

2
1

- Knit on right side
  Purl on wrong side
- Purl on right side
  Knit on wrong side
- Knit tbl on right side
  Purl tbl on wrong side
- K2tog on right side
  P2tog on wrong side
- Ssk on right side
  Ssp on wrong side
- Yarnover
- Make 1
- Slip purlwise with yarn held to wrong side
- Slip 1 stitch to cable needle and hold to back,
  knit 1 tbl from left needle, knit 1 tbl from cable needle
- Slip 1 stitch to cable needle and hold to front,
  knit 1 tbl from left needle, knit 1 tbl from cable needle
- Slip 1 stitch to cable needle and hold to back,
  knit 1 tbl from left needle, purl 1 from cable needle
- Slip 1 stitch to cable needle and hold to front,
  purl 1 from left needle, knit 1 tbl from cable needle
- ← After completion of chart B the first time only:
  Shift beginning of round 9 stitches to left by
  working these stitches.

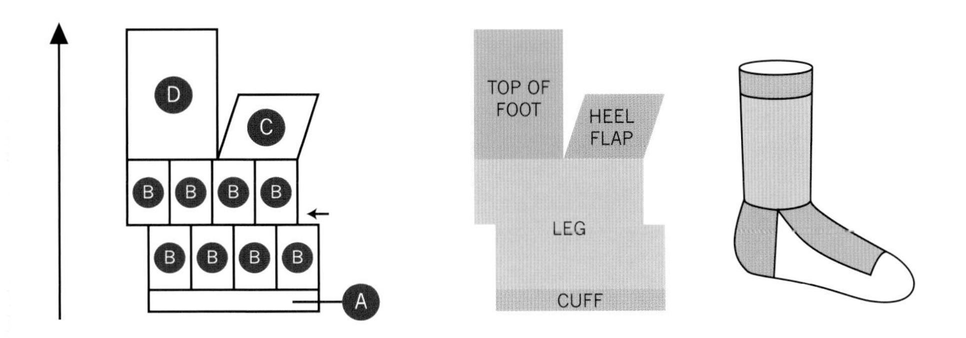

Diagrams represent patterned area of sock which is knit from the cuff toward the toe.
Charts are worked as in diagram.

Gothic Spire

The underlying structure to this sock looks like bricks with each layer of rectangles offset from the layer below. The bobble-like texture is created by wrapping the yarn around the stitches, gathering twisted ribs in a dramatic pattern reminiscent of gothic spires. Despite the staggering of the layers, the ribbing is arranged so that each building block connects to the one below it.

1 CUFF

Cast on 60 [72, 84] stitches and distribute such that each needle has a multiple of 12 stitches. Being careful not to twist, join for working in the round and mark beginning of round (page 168). Work chart A (page 84) for one inch.

2 LEG

Work chart B for 3 vertical repeats, shifting beginning of round 6 stitches to the left each time by working shaded squares. Work chart B once more, but do not shift beginning of round.

3 HEEL FLAP

Divide for heel flap by placing next 30 [36, 42] stitches on hold for top of foot. Heel flap is worked back and forth over remaining 30 [36, 42] stitches. Turn work so that wrong side is facing.

Row 1 (wrong side) Slip 1 purlwise with yarn in front, p29 [35, 41], turn.

Row 2 (right side) (Slip 1 purlwise with yarn in back, k1) 15 [18, 21] times, turn.

Repeat last 2 rows until heel flap measures 2 [2¼, 2½] inches, ending ready to work a right side row.

SIZES
S [M, L] — shown in size M

YARN
Dream In Color Smooshy
100% superwash wool
450 yards per 4 oz
1 skein of In Vino Veritas

NEEDLES
US Size 1 / 2.25mm
or size needed to obtain gauge

NOTIONS
Cable needle, tapestry needle

GAUGE
In stockinette
32 stitches and 48 rows = 4"

In pattern
36 stitches and 48 rows = 4"

MEASUREMENTS

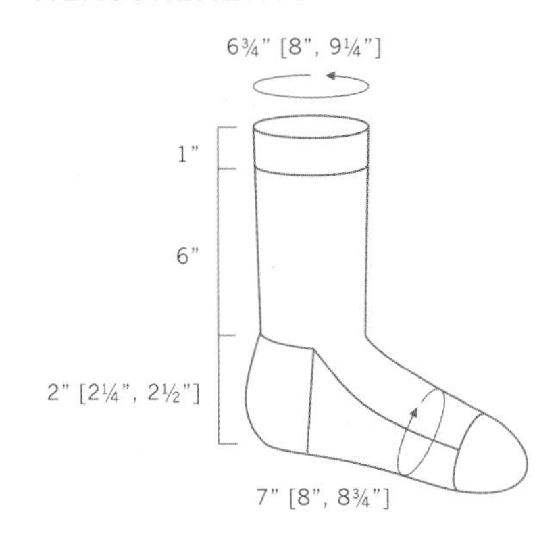

4 TURN HEEL

Continue working back and forth. Use short rows to turn heel as follows:

Row 1 (right side) Slip 1 purlwise with yarn in back, k18 [22, 24], ssk, k1, turn.

Row 2 (wrong side) Slip 1 purlwise with yarn in front, p5 [7, 5], p2tog, p1, turn.

Row 3 Slip 1 purlwise with yarn in back, knit to one stitch before gap caused by turn on previous row, ssk (using one stitch from each side of gap), k1, turn.

Row 4 Slip 1 purlwise with yarn in front, purl to one stitch before gap caused by turn on previous row, p2tog (using one stitch from each side of gap), p1, turn.

Repeat last 2 rows until all heel stitches have been worked, ending ready to work a right side row. 18 [22, 26] heel stitches.

5 FOOT

The following diagrams are used for the top of the foot (see complete instructions below). To read diagrams, begin at the bottom right corner and work left and then up. For example: If working size S, work chart C then chart B twice. After completing charts C and B, work chart B twice then chart D. Then repeat back to the beginning.

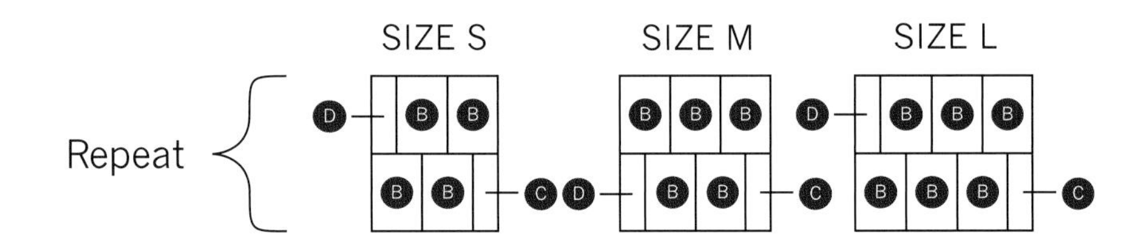

Resume working in the round as follows: Slip 1 purlwise with yarn in back, k8 [10, 12]. Mark beginning of round. Knit remaining heel stitches, pick up and knit into each slipped stitch along edge of heel flap, make 1, mark right side of foot, work held stitches according to diagram, mark left side of foot, make 1, pick up and knit into each slipped stitch along edge of heel flap, knit to end of round.

Right and left side markers divide foot into top of foot section (previously held stitches) and sole. Decrease 2 sole stitches every other round as follows:

Round 1 Knit to 2 stitches before right side of foot, k2tog, work diagram to left side of foot, ssk, knit to end of round. 2 stitches decreased.

Round 2 Knit to right side of foot, work diagram to left side of foot, knit to end of round.

Repeat last 2 rounds until 60 [68, 76] stitches remain—30 [36, 42] top of foot stitches and 30 [32, 34] sole stitches.

Continue working even, without decreasing sole stitches, until foot measures 2 inches less than desired length from back of heel turn.

6 TOE

Keeping pattern centered on top of foot, shift stitches as necessary between top of foot and sole so that each has 30 [34, 38] stitches.

Knit to right side of foot. This is the new beginning of round.

Round 1 Knit to end of round.

Round 2 K1, ssk, knit to 3 stitches before left side of foot, k2tog, k2 (one stitch before and one stitch after left side of foot marker), ssk, knit to 3 stitches before right side of foot, k2tog, k1. 4 stitches decreased.

Repeat last 2 rounds until foot measures desired length, ending after a decrease round. Graft top of foot stitches to sole stitches using Kitchener stitch (page 167). Weave in ends and block.

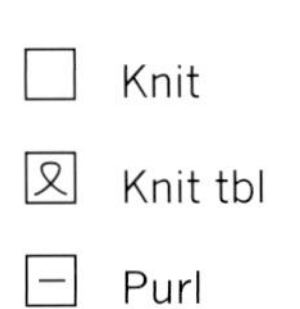

- Knit
- Knit tbl
- Purl
- K2tog
- Ssk
- Yarnover

=4= Wrap yarn twice around 4 stitches: Slip 4 stitches to cable needle and wrap working yarn counterclockwise around slipped stitches twice, then knit 4 stitches from cable needle.

≡4≡ Wrap yarn 4 times around 4 stitches: Slip 4 stitches to cable needle and wrap working yarn counterclockwise around slipped stitches four times, then knit 4 stitches from cable needle..

← Leg section only: Shift beginning of round 6 stitches to left by working these stitches once (do not repeat).

D 6 stitches

1	2	3	4	5	6	Row
–	Q	–	–			18
–	Q	–	–	O	/	17
–	Q	–	–		–	16
–	Q	–	O	/	–	15
–	Q	–		Q	–	14
–	Q	O	/	Q	–	13
–	Q		–	Q	–	12
–	O	/	–	Q	–	11
–		–	–	Q	–	10
–		–	–	Q	–	9
		–	–	Q	–	8
	=4=				–	7
					–	6
					–	5
					–	4
	=4=				–	3
		–	–	Q	–	2
		–	–	Q	–	1

B 12 stitches

1	2	3	4	5	6	7	8	9	10	11	12	Row
						–	Q	–	–			←
		–	–	Q	–	–	Q	–	–			18
\	O	–	–	Q	–	–	Q	–	–	O	/	17
–		–	–	Q	–	–	Q	–	–		–	16
–	\	O	–	Q	–	–	Q	–	O	/	–	15
–	Q		–	Q	–	–	Q	–		Q	–	14
–	Q	\	O	Q	–	–	Q	O	/	Q	–	13
–	Q	–		Q	–	–	Q		–	Q	–	12
–	Q	–	\	O	–	–	O	/	–	Q	–	11
–	Q	–	–		–	–		–	–	Q	–	10
–	Q	–	–	=4=				–	–	Q	–	9
–	Q	–	–					–	–	Q	–	8
–	=4=						=4=				–	7
–											–	6
–				≡4≡							–	5
–											–	4
–	=4=						=4=				–	3
–	Q	–	–					–	–	Q	–	2
–	Q	–	–	=4=				–	–	Q	–	1

C 6 stitches

1	2	3	4	5	6	Row
		–	–	Q	–	18
\	O	–	–	Q	–	17
–		–	–	Q	–	16
–	\	O	–	Q	–	15
–	Q		–	Q	–	14
–	Q	\	O	Q	–	13
–	Q	–		Q	–	12
–	Q	–	\	O	–	11
–	Q	–	–		–	10
–	Q	–	–		–	9
–	Q	–	–			8
–	=4=					7
–						6
–						5
–						4
–	=4=					3
–	Q	–	–			2
–	Q	–	–			1

A 12 stitches

1	2	3	4	5	6	7	8	9	10	11	12	Row
–	Q	–	–	Q	–	–	Q	–	–	Q	–	2
–	Q	–	–	Q	–	–	Q	–	–	Q	–	1

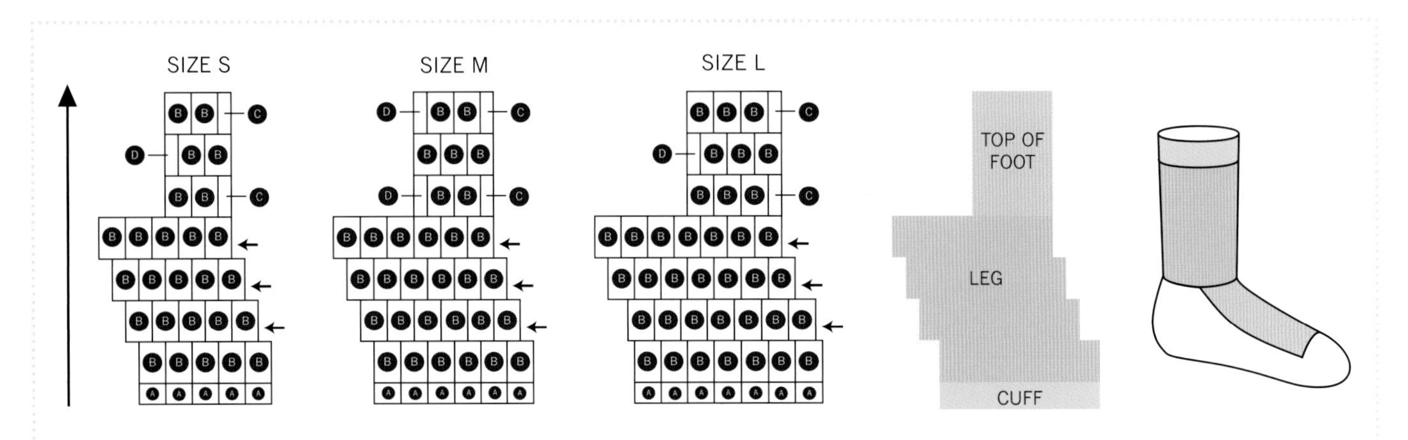

Diagrams represent patterned area of sock which is knit from the cuff toward the toe. Charts are worked as in diagram.

Clandestine

Increasing lace triangles combine with decreasing twisted rib triangles in this skill-building sock. Try your hand at wrapping stitches, changing stitch counts, and four different kinds of decreases. One size is stretchy enough to fit most feet.

0 NOTES

Left and right socks are mirror images of each other. Directions are the same for both socks unless otherwise indicated. When two numbers are given, the first number applies to the left sock and the second number in brackets applies to the right sock.

1 CUFF

Cast on 66 stitches and distribute such that each needle has a multiple of 22 stitches. Being careful not to twist, join for working in the round and mark beginning of round (page 168). Work chart A (page 92) for one inch.

2 LEG

Establish pattern *Work chart B, work chart C. Repeat from * to end of round.

Continue in established pattern through row 14 of charts B and C. Shift beginning of round 14 stitches to the left as follows: K14 and mark new beginning of round.

Work 3 more vertical repeats of charts B and C, shifting beginning of round 14 stitches to left after each vertical repeat.

Work charts B and C once more without shifting beginning of round 14 stitches to the left. Knit 13 [2].

SIZES
One size

YARN
Lorna's Laces Shepherd Sock
80% superwash wool / 20% nylon
215 yards per 2 oz
2 skeins of Cookie's Deep Dark Secret

NEEDLES
US Size 1 / 2.25mm
or size needed to obtain gauge

NOTIONS
Cable needle, tapestry needle

GAUGE
In stockinette
32 stitches and 48 rows = 4"

In pattern
33 stitches and 48 rows = 4"

MEASUREMENTS

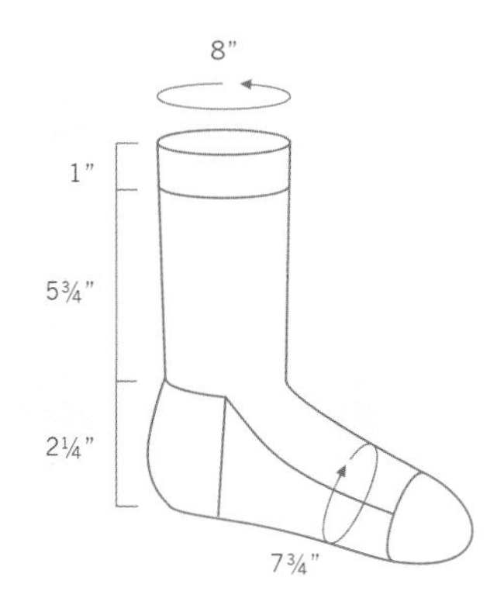

3 HEEL FLAP

Divide for heel flap by placing next 34 stitches on hold for top of foot. Heel flap is worked back and forth over remaining 32 stitches—13 [2] stitches just worked plus 19 [30] stitches from end of previous round. Turn work so that wrong side is facing.

Row 1 (wrong side) Slip 1 purlwise with yarn in front, p31, turn.

Row 2 (right side) (Slip 1 purlwise with yarn in back, k1) 16 times, turn.

Repeat last 2 rows until heel flap measures 2¼ inches, ending ready to work a right side row.

4 TURN HEEL

Continue working back and forth. Use short rows to turn heel as follows:

Row 1 (right side) Slip 1 purlwise with yarn in back, k18, ssk, k1, turn.

Row 2 (wrong side) Slip 1 purlwise with yarn in front, p7, p2tog, p1, turn.

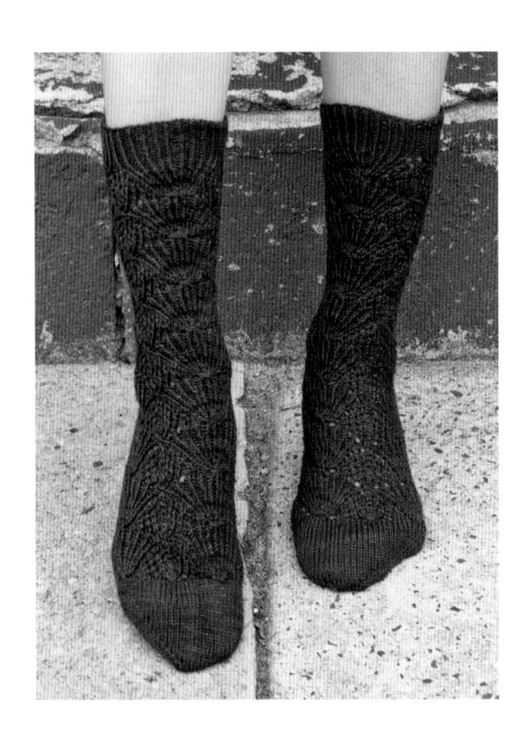

Row 3 Slip 1 purlwise with yarn in back, knit to one stitch before gap caused by turn on previous row, ssk (using one stitch from each side of gap), k1, turn.

Row 4 Slip 1 purlwise with yarn in front, purl to one stitch before gap caused by turn on previous row, p2tog (using one stitch from each side of gap), p1, turn.

Repeat last 2 rows until all heel stitches have been worked, ending ready to work a right side row. 20 heel stitches.

5 FOOT

Resume working in the round as follows: Slip 1 purlwise with yarn in back, k9. Mark beginning of round. Knit remaining heel stitches, pick up and knit into each slipped stitch along edge of heel flap, make 1, mark right side of foot, work as in diagram (page 92) across held stitches, mark left side of foot, make 1, pick up and knit into each slipped stitch along edge of heel flap, knit to end of round.

Right and left side markers divide foot into top of foot section (previously held stitches) and sole. Decrease 2 sole stitches every other round as follows:

Round 1 Knit to 2 stitches before right side of foot, k2tog, work as in diagram to left side of foot, ssk, knit to end of round. 2 stitches decreased.

Round 2 Knit to right side of foot, work as in diagram to left side of foot, knit to end of round.

Repeat last 2 rounds until 30 sole stitches remain. The number of stitches on the top of the foot will vary from row to row.

Continue working even, without decreasing sole stitches, until foot measures no longer than 2 inches less than desired length from back of heel turn, ending with row 14 of charts. 64 stitches.

Knit all stitches until foot measures 2 inches less than desired length.

6 TOE

Keeping pattern centered on top of foot, shift stitches as necessary between top of foot and sole so that each has 32 stitches.

Knit to right side of foot. This is the new beginning of round.

Round 1 Knit to end of round.

Round 2 K1, ssk, knit to 3 stitches before left side of foot, k2tog, k2 (one stitch before and one stitch after left side of foot marker), ssk, knit to 3 stitches before right side of foot, k2tog, k1. 4 stitches decreased.

Repeat last 2 rounds until foot measures desired length, ending after a decrease round. Graft top of foot stitches to sole stitches using Kitchener stitch (page 167). Weave in ends and block.

- Knit
- Knit tbl
- Purl
- Yarnover
- K2tog
- Ssk
- K2tog tbl
- Slip 1 knitwise, k2tog, pass slipped stitch over

- Wrap yarn twice around 2 stitches: Slip 2 stitches to cable needle and wrap working yarn counterclockwise around slipped stitches twice, then knit 2 stitches from cable needle.
- Wrap yarn twice around 3 stitches: Slip 3 stitches to cable needle and wrap working yarn counterclockwise around slipped stitches twice, then knit 3 stitches from cable needle.
- Wrap yarn twice around 5 stitches: Slip 5 stitches to cable needle and wrap working yarn counterclockwise around slipped stitches twice, then knit 5 stitches from cable needle.
- Shift beginning of round 14 stitches to the left by knitting 14 stitches and marking new beginning of round.
- Knit 13 stitches
- Knit 2 stitches

C1

1 stitch before row 1
9 stitches after row 14

C2

1 stitch before row 1
9 stitches after row 14

B1

11 stitches before row 1
3 stitches after row 14

B2

11 stitches before row 1
3 stitches after row 14

C

1 stitch before row 1
17 stitches after row 14

B

21 stitches before row 1
5 stitches after row 14

A

22 stitches

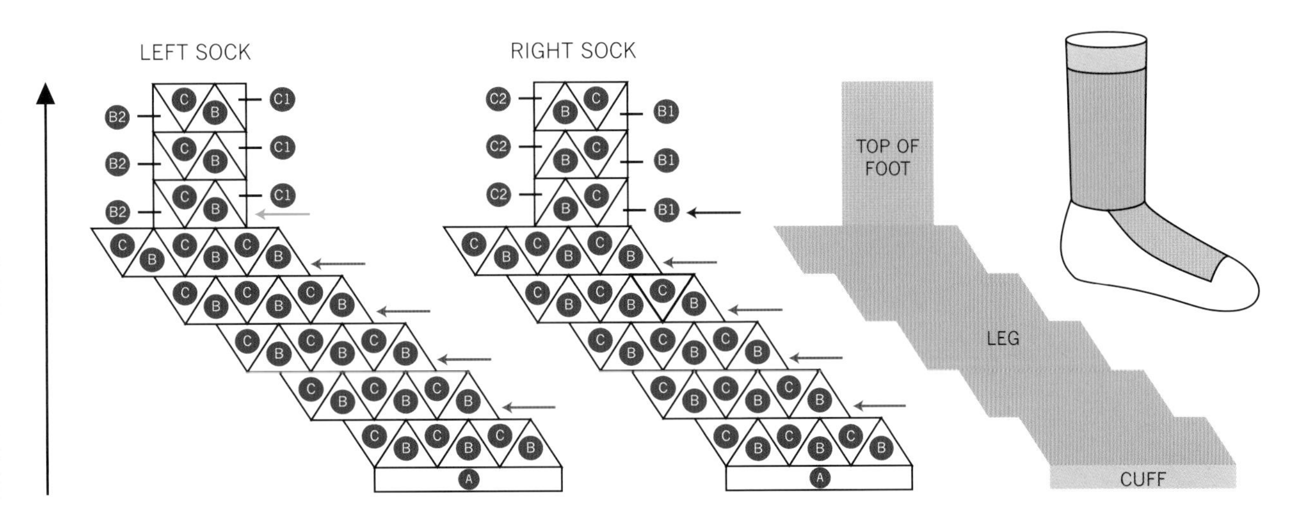

Diagrams represent patterned area of sock which is knit from the cuff toward the toe. Charts are worked as in diagram.

Wedge

This sock combines short-row trapezoids and rectangles to give the appearance of stockinette bands separated by garter stitch wedges. Don't be intimidated by the diagram, this sock is super easy to knit and involves minimal purling. When working short rows in garter stitch, it's unnecessary to pick up wraps, and grafting in garter stitch is the same as in stockinette.

1 CUFF

Cast on 48 [56, 64, 72, 80] stitches and distribute such that each needle has a multiple of 6 [7, 8, 9, 10] stitches. Being careful not to twist, join for working in the round and mark beginning of round (page 168).

Round 1 Knit to end of round.

Round 2 Knit to end of round.

Round 3 Purl to end of round.

Repeat last two rounds for ½ inch, ending after a purl round.

2 LEG

Work (Increase Wedge, Stockinette Band, Decrease Wedge) 3 or 4 times depending on yarn amount (Version 1 uses 4 repeats, and Version 2 uses 3) as follows.

INCREASE WEDGE

Work back and forth using short rows.

Row 1 (right side) K12 [14, 16, 18, 20], wrap and turn (page 167).

Row 2 (wrong side) K18 [21, 24, 27, 30], wrap and turn.

Row 3 (right side) K24 [28, 32, 36, 40], wrap and turn.

Row 4 (wrong side) K30 [35, 40, 45, 50], wrap and turn.

Row 5 (right side) K36 [42, 48, 54, 60], wrap and turn.

Row 6 (wrong side) K42 [49, 56, 63, 70], wrap and turn.

Place marker for beginning of round, with last wrapped stitch to the right of marker.

SIZES
XS [S, M, L, XL] — shown in size M

YARN
Version 1 Hand Jive Knits
Nature's Palette Fingering
100% merino wool
185 yards per 50g
2 skeins of Seafoam

Version 2 Blue Moon Fiber Arts
Socks That Rock Lightweight
100% superwash wool
360 yards per 4.5 oz
1 skein of Mr. Green Jeans

NEEDLES
US Size 1 / 2.25mm
or size needed to obtain gauge

NOTIONS
Stitch marker, tapestry needle

GAUGE
In stockinette
32 stitches and 48 rows = 4"

In pattern
32 stitches and 48 rows = 4"

MEASUREMENTS

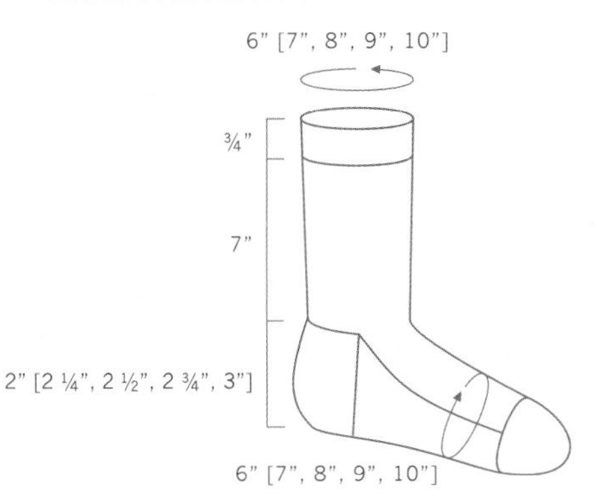

Next round Knit to 2 stitches before marker, make 1, k2tog.

Next round Purl to end of round.

STOCKINETTE BAND

Knit 12 rounds. Remove marker, k24 [28, 32, 36, 40], place marker for beginning of round.

Next round Purl to end of round.

DECREASE WEDGE

Remove marker and work back and forth using short rows.

Row 1 (right side) K42 [49, 56, 63, 70], wrap and turn.

Row 2 (wrong side) K36 [42, 48, 54, 60], wrap and turn.

Row 3 (right side) K30 [35, 40, 45, 50], wrap and turn.

Row 4 (wrong side) K24 [28, 32, 36, 40], wrap and turn.

Row 5 (right side) K18 [21, 24, 27, 30], wrap and turn.

Row 6 (wrong side) K12 [14, 16, 18, 20], wrap and turn.

3 HEEL SET-UP

Work Increase Wedge and Stockinette Band.

GARTER STITCH SHORT ROWS
Working short rows in garter stitch is easy because there's no need to pick up wraps.

KITCHENER STITCH
Working Kitchener stitch in garter stitch is the same as in stockinette.

4 HEEL

Remove marker and work back and forth using short rows.

Row 1 (right side) K42 [49, 56, 63, 70], wrap and turn.

Row 2 (wrong side) K36 [42, 48, 54, 60], wrap and turn.

Row 3 (right side) K33 [38, 44, 49, 55], wrap and turn.

Row 4 (wrong side) K30 [34, 40, 44, 50], wrap and turn.

Next row Knit to 1 stitch before wrapped stitch, wrap and turn.

Repeat last row 19 [21, 25, 29, 33] more times so that the last row worked is on the wrong side: K10 [12, 14, 14, 16], wrap and turn. 11 [12, 14, 16, 18] stitches wrapped per side.

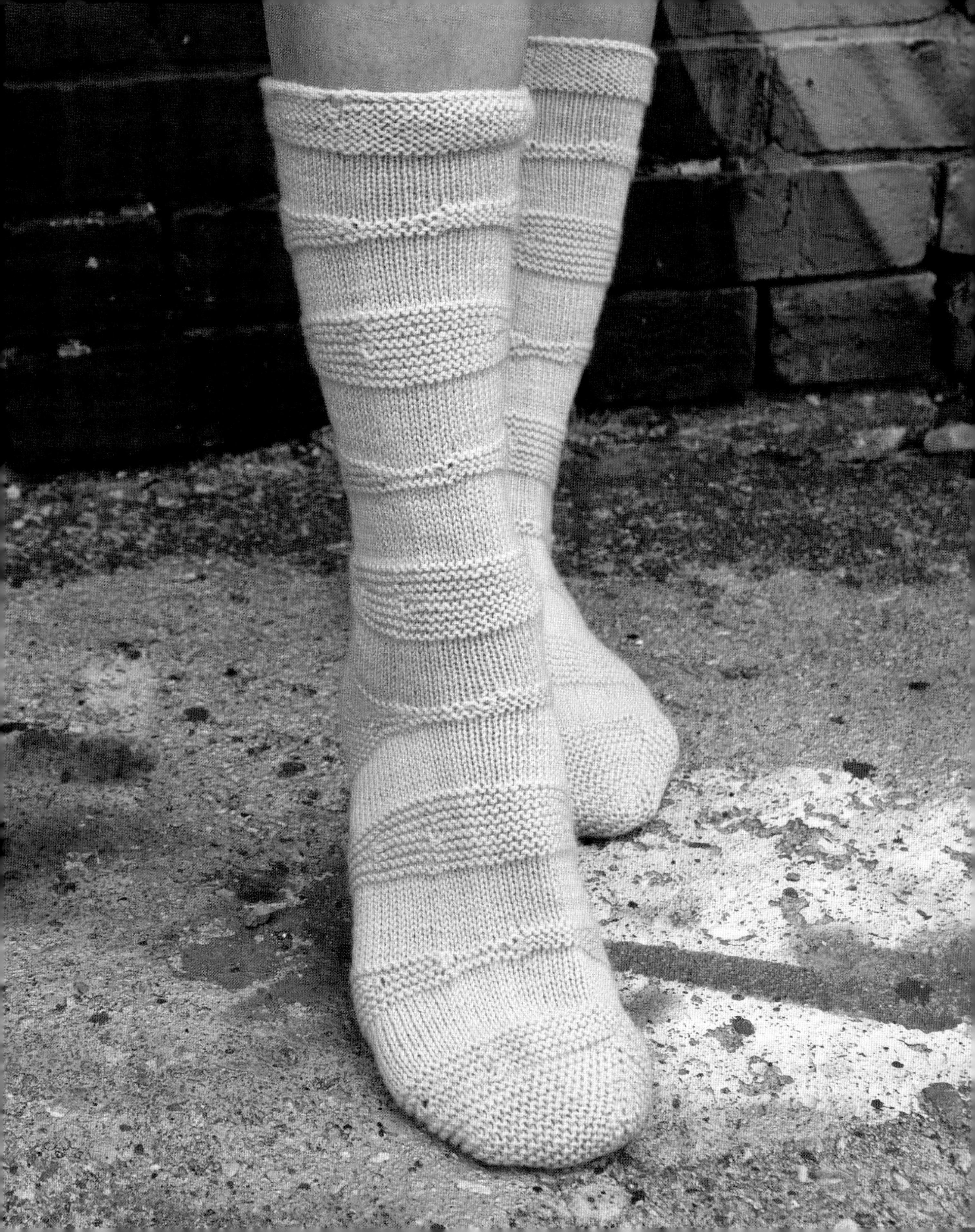

Next row (right side) Knit up to and including first wrapped stitch, wrap and turn. (That stitch is double wrapped.)

Repeat last row 19 [21, 25, 29, 33] more times so that the last row worked is on the wrong side: K30 [34, 40, 44, 50], wrap and turn.

Next row (right side) K33 [38, 44, 49, 55], wrap and turn.

Next row (wrong side) K42 [49, 56, 63, 70], wrap and turn.

Place marker for beginning of round.

Next round Knit to 2 stitches before marker, make 1, k2tog.

Next round Purl one round.

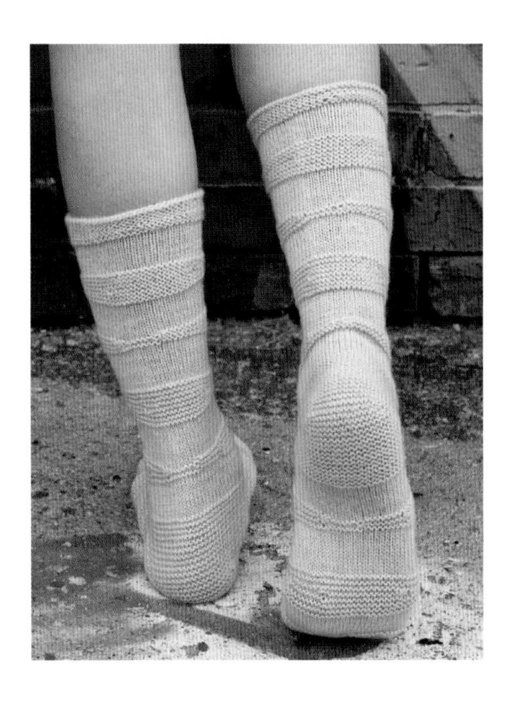

5 FOOT

Work Stockinette Band and Decrease Wedge.

Work (Increase Wedge, Stockinette Band, Decrease Wedge) until foot measures as close to, but not longer than 2 inches less than desired length of foot, ending after Decrease Wedge.

If beginning of round is on top of foot, remove marker, k24 [28, 32, 36, 40] and mark new beginning of round.

Round 1 Knit to end of round.

Round 2 Purl to end of round.

Repeat last 2 rounds until foot measures 2 inches less than desired length, ending with a purl round.

Remove marker, k18 [21, 24, 27, 30], place marker for beginning of round now at side of foot.

6 TOE

Toe is worked back and forth using short rows.

Row 1 (right side) K24 [28, 32, 36, 40], wrap and turn.

Row 2 (wrong side) K24 [28, 32, 36, 40], wrap and turn.

Next row Knit to 1 stitch before first wrapped stitch, wrap and turn.

Repeat last row 15 [17, 21, 23, 25] more times. 8 [10, 10, 12, 14] unwrapped stitches in the center of the toe. 9 [10, 12, 13, 14] wrapped stitches on either side.

Next row Knit up to and including first wrapped stitch, wrap and turn. Next stitch is now double wrapped.

Repeat last row 15 [17, 21, 23, 25] more times.

Graft toe stitches to top of foot stitches using Kitchener stitch (page 167). Weave in ends and block.

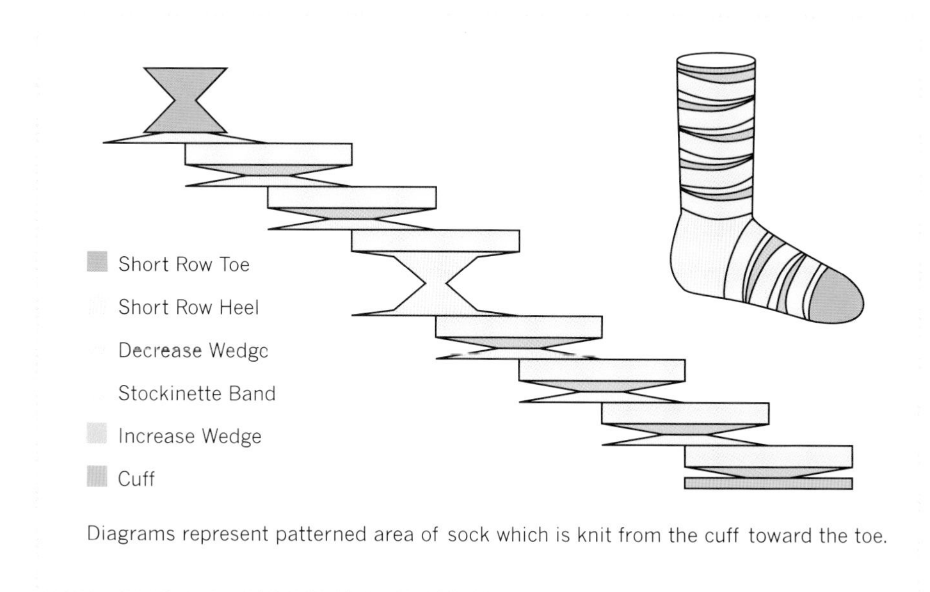

Diagrams represent patterned area of sock which is knit from the cuff toward the toe.

CHAPTER 3

DIAGONALS

I've always been drawn to things that go off the grid, whether they are knitting designs or choose-your-own-adventure road trips. Diagonal patterns within the knitted fabric can be created using different methods: cabling (Sake), lace (Cusp), or using panels that travel with paired increases and decreases (Thelonious). Elements that travel off the grid can take a variety

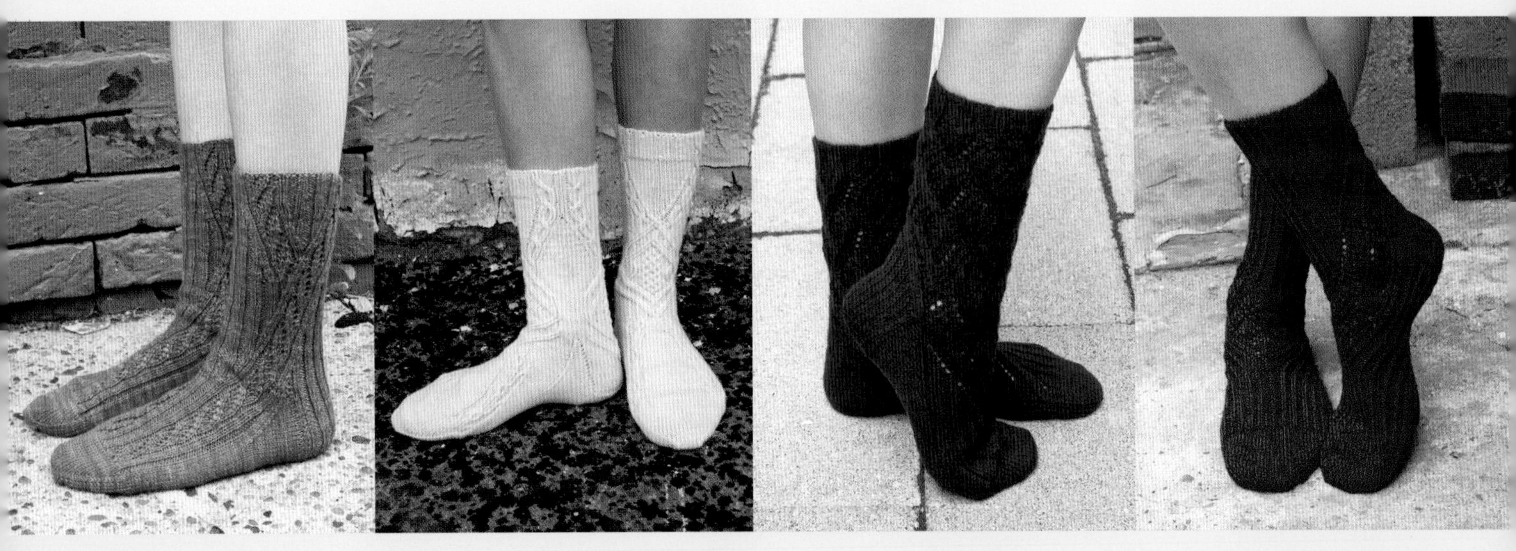

Thelonious Stricken In and Out Cusp

of paths by zigging and zagging back and forth (In and Out), intersecting with other diagonal elements (Thelonious), colliding into large objects or motifs (Stricken), or simply shooting straight off in one direction and never wavering (German Stocking). These adventurous travelers can have serene landscapes of stockinette (Stricken), slightly textured terrain (Cusp), or wild untamed lace (Pointelle).

With diagonals, new shapes can be created and boundaries pushed. Here begins exploration into new territory.

Pointelle Pointelle Sake German Stocking

Thelonious

Simple lace panels angle over a ribbed background, wrapping around the leg and foot. Four panels become two as they collide, forming Y intersections. While each individual component is quite simple, the pattern as a whole has many moving parts. Stitch markers will help keep your place.

1 CUFF

Cast on 56 [64, 72, 80] stitches. Being careful not to twist, join for working in the round and mark beginning of round (page 168). Establish pattern as follows: *P1, place marker, work chart A (page 108), place marker, (k1, p2, k1) 2 [3, 4, 5] times, place marker, work chart B, place marker, p1, place marker. Repeat from * to end of round. There are 10 markers: A1, A2, B1, B2, S (marking halfway through round), A3, A4, B3, B4, and E (marking end of round).

Work in established pattern until cuff measures approximately 1¾ [1, 1¼, ½] inches, ending after row 1 [3, 5, 7] of charts A and B.

2 LEG WITH FOUR PANELS

Round 1 (Travel Round) *Work stitches as set (see sidebar on page 104) to A1 marker, make 1 right in 2x2 rib (see sidebar on page 104), slip A1 marker, work chart A, slip A2 marker, ssk, work stitches as set to 2 stitches before B1 marker, k2tog, slip B1 marker, work chart B, slip B2 marker, make 1 left in 2x2 rib, work stitches as set to S marker. Repeat from * to end of round, except substitute A1, A2, B1, B2, and S with A3, A4, B3, B4 and E respectively.

Rounds 2-4 (Straight Rounds) *Work stitches as set to A1 marker, slip A1 marker, work chart A, slip A2 marker, work stitches as set to B1 marker, slip B1 marker, work chart B, slip B2 marker, work stitches as set to S marker. Repeat from * to end of round, except substitute A1, A2, B1, B2, and S with A3, A4, B3, B4 and E respectively.

Continue traveling every 4th round until 2 stitches remain between A2 and B1 markers, ending after a Travel Round.

SIZES
XS [S, M, L] — shown in size S

YARN
Koigu Premium Merino (KPM)
100% merino wool
175 yards per 50g
2 [2, 3, 3] skeins of color #2330

NEEDLES
US Size 1 / 2.25mm
or size needed to obtain gauge

NOTIONS
Tapestry needle, 10 stitch markers

GAUGE
In stockinette
32 stitches and 48 rows = 4"

In pattern
32 stitches and 48 rows = 4"

MEASUREMENTS

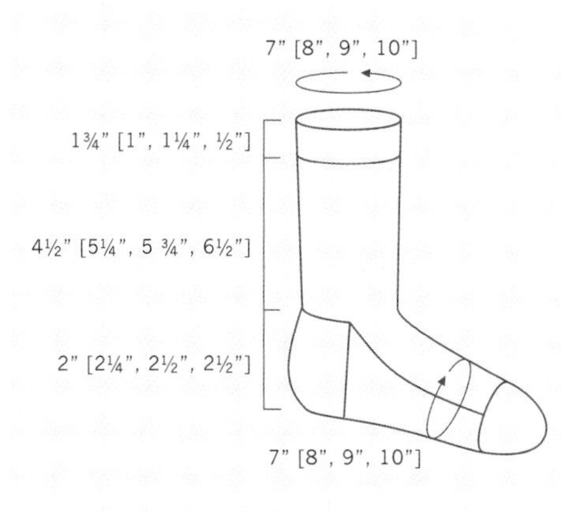

3 LEG WITH TWO FULL PANELS AND TWO DECREASING PANELS

Remove B1 and A4 markers, rename B2 marker as D marker, and rename A3 marker as C marker. 8 stitch markers remain.

Begin working charts C and D as follows:

Rounds 1-3 (Straight Rounds) Work stitches as set to A1 marker, slip A1 marker, work chart A, slip A2 marker, work chart D, slip D marker, work stitches as set to S marker, slip S marker, work stitches as set to C marker, slip C marker, work chart C, slip B3 marker, work chart B, slip B4 marker, work stitches as set to end of round.

Round 4 (Travel Round) Work stitches as set to A1 marker, make 1 right in 2x2 rib, slip A1 marker, work chart A, slip A2 marker, work chart D, slip D marker, make 1 left in 2x2 rib, work stitches as set to S marker, slip S marker, work stitches as set to C marker, make 1 right in 2x2 rib, slip C marker, work chart C, slip B3 marker, work chart B, slip B4 marker, make 1 left in 2x2 rib, work stitches as set to end of round.

Continue in established pattern, working Travel Round every 4th round through end of charts C and D.

WORK STITCHES AS SET
Work the current stitch on the left needle depending on how it looks: Knit the knits, k2tog's, and ssk's. Purl the purl stitches.

MAKE 1 RIGHT IN 2X2 RIB
To increase at the end of 2x2 rib, use a right leaning increase. If the second to last stitch worked was a purl stitch, make 1 knit right. Otherwise, make 1 purl right.

MAKE 1 LEFT IN 2X2 RIB
To increase at the beginning of 2x2 rib, use a left leaning increase. If the second stitch on the left needle is a purl stitch, make 1 knit left. Otherwise, make 1 purl left.

4 LEG WITH TWO PANELS

Remove C and D markers. 6 stitch markers remain.

Rounds 1-3 (Straight Rounds) Work stitches as set to A1 marker, slip A1 marker, work chart A, slip A2 marker, work stitches as set to S marker, slip S marker, work stitches as set to B3 marker, slip B3 marker, work chart B, slip B4 marker, work stitches as set to end of round.

Round 4 (Travel Round) Work stitches as set to A1 marker, make 1 right in 2x2 rib, slip A1 marker, work chart A, slip A2 marker, ssk, work stitches as set to S marker, slip S marker, work stitches as set to 2 stitches before B3 marker, k2tog, slip B3 marker, work chart B, slip B4 marker, make 1 left in 2x2 rib, work stitches as set to end of round.

Continue in established pattern, working Travel Round every 4th round, until there are 15 [17, 19, 21] stitches between beginning of round and A1 marker, ending after a Travel Round. Work one more Straight Round.

5 HEEL FLAP

Work 14 [16, 18, 20] stitches as set. Divide for heel flap by placing next 28 [32, 36, 40] stitches on hold for top of foot. Heel flap is worked back and forth over remaining 28 [32, 36, 40] stitches — 14 [16, 18, 20] stitches just worked plus 14 [16, 18, 20] stitches from end of previous round. Turn work so that wrong side is facing.

Row 1 (wrong side) Slip 1 purlwise with yarn in front, work 26 [30, 34, 38] stitches as set, p1, turn.

Row 2 (right side) Slip 1 purlwise with yarn in back, work 26 [30, 34, 38] stitches as set, k1, turn.

Repeat last 2 rows until heel flap measures 2 [2¼, 2½, 2½] inches, ending ready to work a right side row.

6 TURN HEEL

Continue working back and forth. Use short rows to turn heel as follows:

Row 1 (right side) Slip 1 purlwise with yarn in back, k16 [18, 20, 22], ssk, k1, turn.

Row 2 (wrong side) Slip 1 purlwise with yarn in front, p7, p2tog, p1, turn.

Row 3 Slip 1 purlwise with yarn in back, knit to one stitch before gap caused by turn on previous row, ssk (using one stitch from each side of gap), k1, turn.

Row 4 Slip 1 purlwise with yarn in front, purl to gap one stitch before caused by turn on previous row, p2tog (using one stitch from each side of gap), p1, turn.

Repeat last 2 rows until all heel stitches have been worked, ending ready to work a right side row. 18 [20, 22, 24] heel stitches.

7 FOOT

Resume working in the round as follows: Slip 1 purlwise with yarn in back, k8 [9, 10, 11]. Mark beginning of round. Knit remaining heel stitches, pick up and knit into each slipped stitch along edge of heel flap, make 1, mark right side of foot, work held stitches in established traveling pattern, mark left side of foot, make 1, pick up and knit into each slipped stitch along edge of heel flap, knit to end of round.

627-2720 627-2

Right and left side of foot markers divide foot into top of foot section (previously held stitches) and sole.

Round 1 Knit to 2 stitches before right side of foot, k2tog, work established pattern across top of foot (traveling every 4th round), ssk, knit to end of round. 2 stitches decreased.

Round 2 Knit to right side of foot, work established pattern across top of foot, knit to end of round.

Decrease 2 sole stitches every other round until 56 [64, 72, 80] stitches remain—28 [32, 36, 40] top of foot stitches and 28 [32, 36, 40] sole stitches AND AT THE SAME TIME work established pattern (traveling every 4th round) across top of foot until 4 stitches remain between A2 and B3 markers. Once 56 [64, 72, 80] stitches remain, continue working even without decreasing sole stitches. Once 4 stitches remain between A2 and B3 markers, continue in established pattern on top of foot without traveling.

Work as above until foot measures 2 inches less than desired length from back of heel turn.

8 TOE

Knit to right side of foot. This is the new beginning of round.

Round 1 Knit to end of round.

Round 2 K1, ssk, knit to 3 stitches before left side of foot, k2tog, k2 (one stitch before and one stitch after left side of foot marker), ssk, knit to 3 stitches before right side of foot, k2tog, k1. 4 stitches decreased.

Repeat last 2 rounds until foot measures desired length, ending after a decrease round. Graft top of foot stitches to sole stitches using Kitchener stitch (page 167). Weave in ends and block.

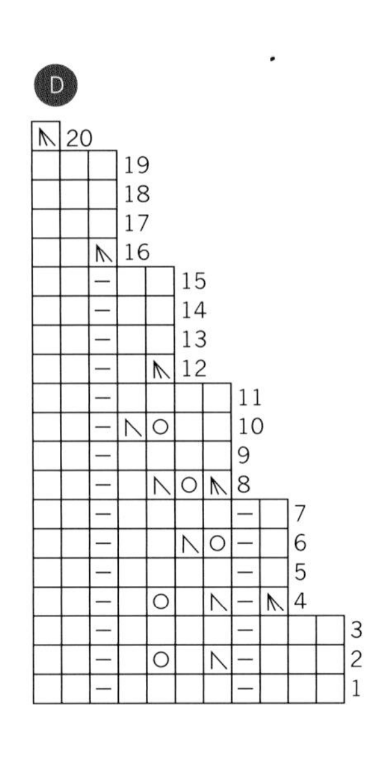

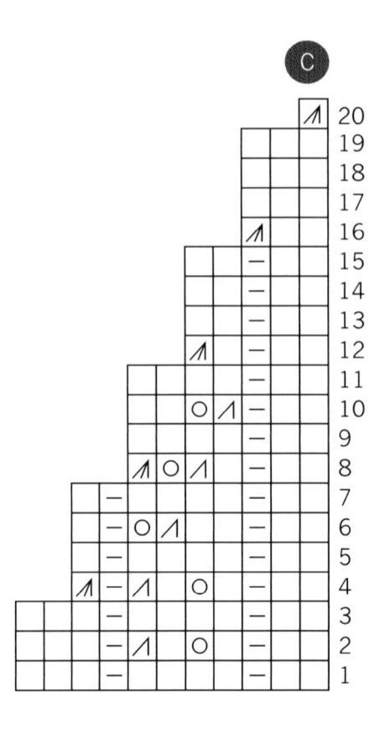

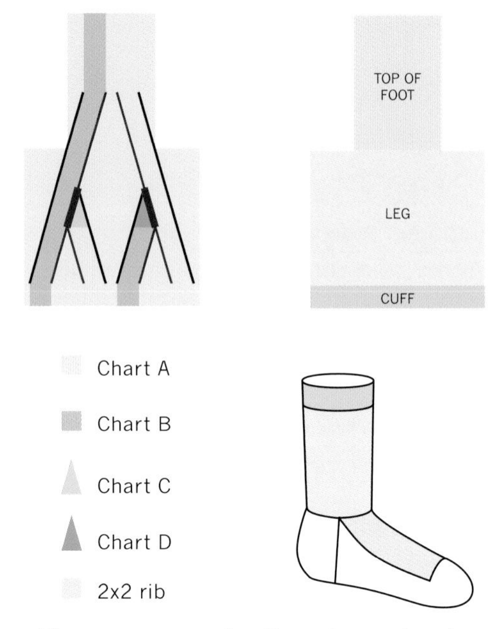

Diagrams represent patterned area of sock which is knit from the cuff toward the toe. Charts are worked as in diagram.

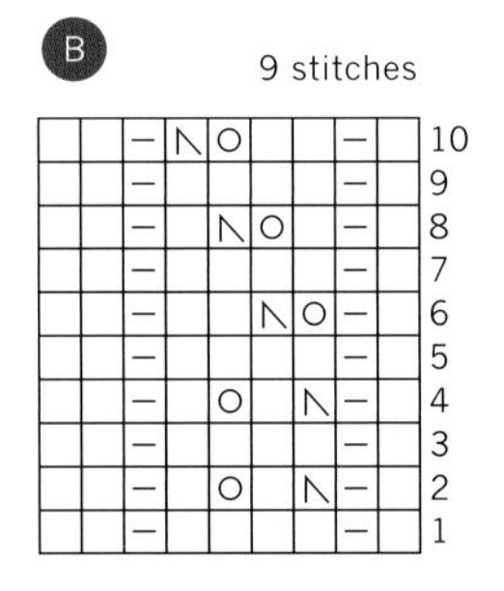

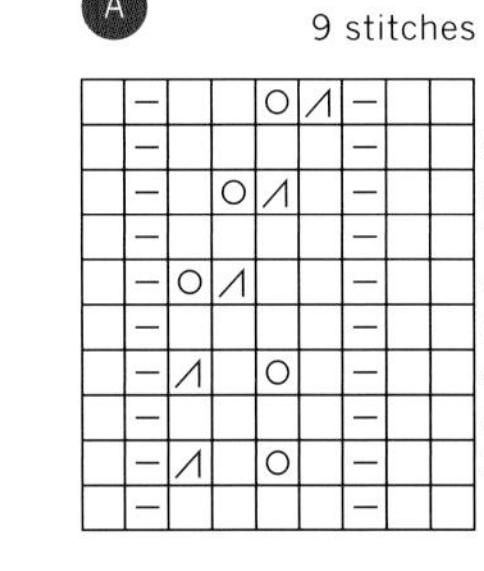

- Knit
- Purl
- Yarnover
- Ssk
- Sssk
- K2tog
- K3tog

/ Increase in 2x2 rib every 4th row, immediately after marker, as follows: If 2nd stitch on left needle is a purl stitch, make 1 knit left. Otherwise, make 1 purl left.

\ Increase in 2x2 rib every 4th row, immediately before marker, as follows: If 2nd stitch on right needle is a purl stitch, make 1 knit right. Otherwise, make 1 purl right.

/ Decrease 1 stitch every 4th row by knitting two stitches before marker together.

\ Decrease 1 stitch every 4th row by working ssk immediately after marker.

/ Decrease 2 stitches every 4th row by knitting three stitches together within chart C.

\ Decrease 2 stitches every 4th row by working sssk within chart D.

Stricken

Large twisted stitch motifs cover the front and back of the leg of these socks. Two panels angle inward and converge at the motif while two different panels emerge from it and travel away from each other. Named after the German word for knitting, the twisted stitch style is like that used in traditional German knitting.

1 CUFF

Cast on 64 [72, 80, 88] stitches. Being careful not to twist, join for working in the round and mark beginning of round (page 168). Work chart A (page 117), place marker, work chart B over 14 [18, 22, 26] stitches by repeating marked section 3 [4, 5, 6] times, place marker, work chart C, place marker, work chart A, place marker, work chart B over 14 [18, 22, 26] stitches by repeating marked section 3 [4, 5, 6] times, place marker, work chart C. There are 6 markers: A1, C1, S (marking halfway point), A2, C2, and end of round. Slip markers as they are encountered unless otherwise noted. Continue in established pattern for 1¼ [¾, 1, 1¼] inch(es), ending after row 7 [1, 4, 7] of charts.

2 LEG

Begin traveling as follows:

Round 1 Work chart A, knit to C1 marker, work chart C, work chart A, knit to C2 marker, work chart C.

Round 2 Make 1 right, place marker (label this A1+), work chart A, ssk, knit to 2 stitches before C1 marker, k2tog, work chart C, slip S marker, make 1 right, place marker (label this A2+), work chart A, ssk, knit to 2 stitches before C2 marker, k2tog, work chart C. 62 [70, 78, 86] stitches.

SIZES
XS [S, M, L] — shown in size S

YARN
Claudia Hand Painted Yarns
Fingering
100% superwash merino wool
175 yards per 50g
2 [2, 3, 3] skeins of Canary

NEEDLES
US Size 1 / 2.25mm
or size needed to obtain gauge

NOTIONS
Cable needle, 10 stitch markers, tapestry needle

GAUGE
In stockinette
32 stitches and 48 rows = 4"

In pattern
36 stitches and 48 rows = 4"

MEASUREMENTS

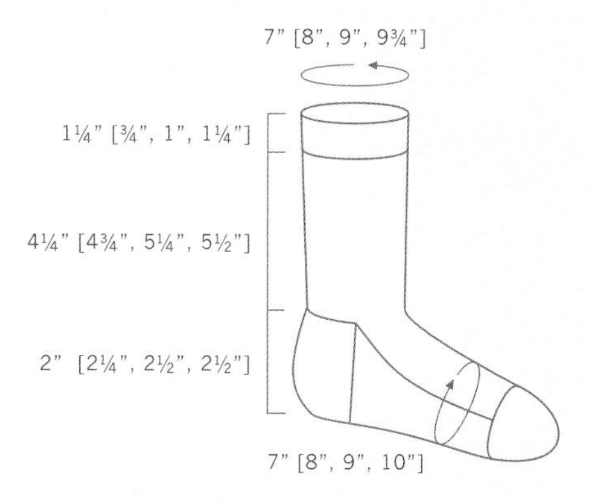

Round 3 Knit 1, slip A1+ marker, work chart A, knit to C1 marker, work chart C, place marker (leaving S marker on left needle, and label new marker as C1+), make 1 left before S marker, slip S marker, knit 1, slip A2+ marker, work chart A, knit to C2 marker, work chart C, place marker (label this C2+), make 1 left before end of round. 64 [72, 80, 88] stitches. There are 10 markers: A1+, A1, C1, C1+, S, A2+, A2, C2, C2+, and end of round. Increases will occur next to markers with + signs.

Rounds 4 and 5 (Straight Rounds) Knit to A1+ marker, work chart A, knit to C1 marker, work chart C, knit to A2+ marker, work chart A, knit to C2 marker, work chart C, knit to end of round.

Round 6 (Travel Round) Knit to A1+ marker, make 1 right before A1+ marker, work chart A, ssk, knit to 2 stitches before C1 marker, k2tog, work chart C, slip C1+ marker, make 1 left, knit to A2+ marker, make 1 right before A2+ marker, work chart A, ssk, knit to 2 stitches before C2 marker, k2tog, work chart C, slip C2+ marker, make 1 left, knit to end of round.

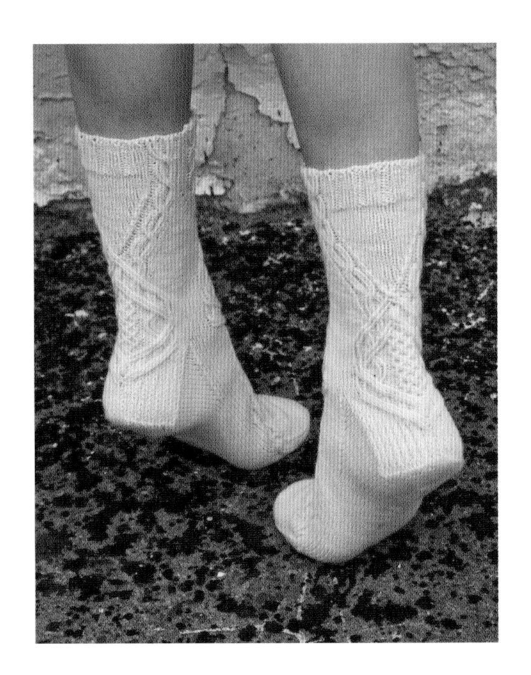

Repeat last 3 rounds, traveling every third round, until 2 stitches remain between A1 and C1 markers, ending after row 7 of charts A and C.

3 LEG MOTIF

Remove stitch markers and work chart D for 34 rounds. 72 [80, 88, 96] stitches.

4 HEEL FLAP

Divide for heel flap by placing previous 36 [40, 44, 48] stitches on hold for top of foot. Work chart E (page 119) back and forth over remaining 36 [40, 44, 48] stitches for heel flap, repeating last two rows until heel flap measures 2 [2¼, 2½, 2½] inches. 30 [34, 38, 42] heel stitches.

5 TURN HEEL

Continue working back and forth. Use short rows to turn heel as follows:

Row 1 (right side) Slip 1 purlwise with yarn in back, k16 [18, 20, 22], ssk, k1, turn.

Row 2 (wrong side) Slip 1 purlwise with yarn in front, p5, p2tog, p1, turn.

Row 3 Slip 1 purlwise with yarn in back, knit to one stitch before gap caused by turn on previous row, ssk (using one stitch from each side of gap), k1, turn.

Row 4 Slip 1 purlwise with yarn in front, purl to one stitch before gap caused by turn on previous row, p2tog (using one stitch from each side of gap), p1, turn.

Repeat last 2 rows until all heel stitches have been worked, ending ready to work a right side row. 18 [20, 22, 24] heel stitches.

6 GUSSET SHAPING

Gusset shaping is worked AT THE SAME TIME as Top of Foot. See directions for Top of Foot in section 7.

Resume working in the round as follows: Slip 1 purlwise with yarn in back, k8 [9, 10, 11]. Mark beginning of round. Knit remaining heel stitches, pick up and knit into each slipped stitch along edge of heel flap, make 1, mark right side of foot, work Top of Foot (see section 7) across held stitches, mark left side of foot, make 1, pick up and knit into each slipped stitch along edge of heel flap, knit to end of round.

Right and left side markers divide foot into top of foot section (previously held stitches) and sole. Decrease 2 sole stitches every other round as follows:

Round 1 Knit to 2 stitches before right side of foot, k2tog, work Top of Foot to left side of foot, ssk, knit to end of round. 2 stitches decreased.

Round 2 Knit to right side of foot, work Top of Foot to left side of foot, knit to end of round. Repeat last 2 rounds until 28 [32, 36, 40] sole stitches remain. Stitch count across top of foot will vary. Continue working even, without decreasing sole stitches, until foot measures 2 inches less than desired length from back of heel turn. Proceed to Toe.

7 TOP OF FOOT

The following directions are for the Top of Foot which is worked at the same time as Gusset Shaping (above).

Work chart F for 16 rows. 30 [34, 38, 42] top of foot stitches.

Begin working chart G as follows:

Row 1 Knit 4 [6, 8, 10], k2tog, place marker, work chart G, k1, place marker, make 1 right, place marker, k1, work chart G, place marker, ssk, knit remaining top of foot stitches. 29 [33, 37, 41] top of foot stitches. There are 4 markers across top of foot: G1, G1+, G2+, and G2.

Row 2 Knit to G1 marker, work chart G, k1, slip G1+ marker, make 1 left, k1, slip G2+ marker, k1, work chart G, slip G2 marker, knit remaining top of foot stitches. 30 [34, 38, 42] top of foot stitches.

Rows 3 and 4 (Straight Rows) Knit to G1 marker, work chart G, k1, slip G1+ marker, knit to G2+ marker, k1, work chart G, slip G2 marker, knit remaining top of foot stitches.

Row 5 (Travel Row) Knit to 2 stitches before G1 marker, k2tog, work chart G, k1, slip G1+ marker, make 1 left, knit to G2+ marker, make 1 right before G2+ marker, k1, work chart G, slip G2 marker, ssk, knit remaining top of foot stitches.

Continue in established pattern, traveling every 4th row by alternating 3 Straight Rows and 1 Travel Row, until 2 stitches remain before first G1 marker. Continue working straight without traveling.

8 TOE

Knit to right side of foot. This is the new beginning of round.

Set-up Round K1, ssk, knit to 3 stitches before left side of foot, k2tog, knit to end of round. 2 stitches decreased. 56 [64, 72, 80] stitches divided evening between top of foot and sole.

Round 1 Knit to end of round.

Round 2 K1, ssk, knit to 3 stitches before left side of foot, k2tog, k2 (one stitch before and one stitch after left side of foot marker), ssk, knit to 3 stitches before right side of foot, k2tog, k1. 4 stitches decreased.

Repeat last 2 rounds until foot measures desired length, ending after a decrease round. Graft top of foot stitches to sole stitches using Kitchener stitch (page 167). Weave in ends and block.

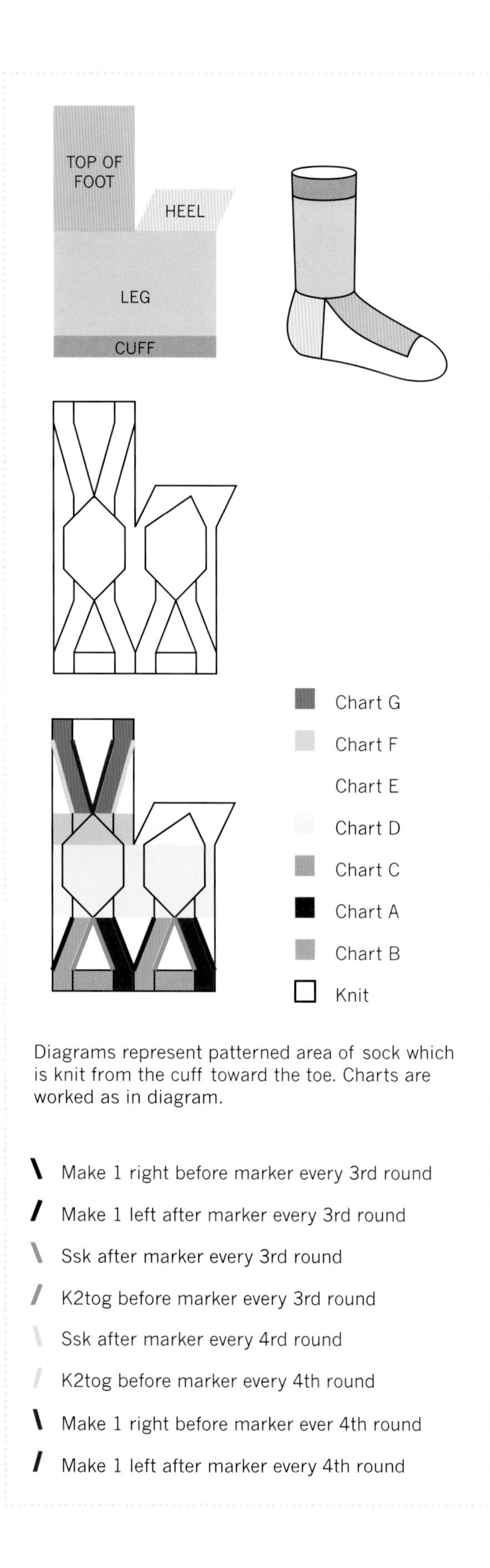

Diagrams represent patterned area of sock which is knit from the cuff toward the toe. Charts are worked as in diagram.

- Make 1 right before marker every 3rd round
- Make 1 left after marker every 3rd round
- Ssk after marker every 3rd round
- K2tog before marker every 3rd round
- Ssk after marker every 4rd round
- K2tog before marker every 4th round
- Make 1 right before marker ever 4th round
- Make 1 left after marker every 4th round

On right side: Knit
On wrong side: Purl

On right side: Purl
On wrong side: Knit

On right side: Knit tbl
On wrong side: Purl tbl

On right side: K2tog
On wrong side: P2tog

On right side: Ssk
On wrong side: Ssp

Make 1 right

Make 1 left

Slip purlwise with yarn held to wrong side of work

On right side: Slip 1 to cable needle and hold to front, k1 tbl from left needle, k1 tbl from cable needle.
On wrong side: Slip 1 to cable needle and hold to front, p1 tbl from left needle, p1 tbl from cable needle.

On right side: Slip 1 to cable needle and hold to back, k1 tbl from left needle, k1 tbl from cable needle.
On wrong side: Slip 1 to cable needle and hold to back, p1 tbl from left needle, p1 tbl from cable needle.

On right side: Slip 1 to cable needle and hold to front, k1 from left needle, k1 tbl from cable needle.
On wrong side: Slip 1 to cable needle and hold to front, p1 tbl from left needle, p1 from cable needle.

On right side: Slip 1 to cable needle and hold to back, k1 tbl from left needle, k1 from cable needle.
On wrong side: Slip 1 to cable needle and hold to back, p1 from left needle, p1 tbl from cable needle.

On right side: Slip 1 to cable needle and hold to front, p1 from left needle, k1 tbl from cable needle.
On wrong side: Slip 1 to cable needle and hold to front, p1 tbl from left needle, k1 from cable needle.

On right side: Slip 1 to cable needle and hold to back, k1 tbl from left needle, p1 from cable needle.
On wrong side: Slip 1 to cable needle and hold to back, k1 from left needle, p1 tbl from cable needle.

On right side: Slip 2 to cable needle and hold to front, p1 from left needle, k2 tbl from cable needle.

On right side: Slip 1 to cable needle and hold to back, k2 tbl from left needle, p1 from cable needle.

On right side: Slip 2 to cable needle and hold to front, k2 tbl from left needle, k2 tbl from cable needle.

On right side: Slip 2 to cable needle and hold to back, k2 tbl from left needle, k2 tbl from cable needle.

D

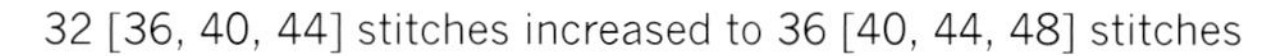

32 [36, 40, 44] stitches increased to 36 [40, 44, 48] stitches

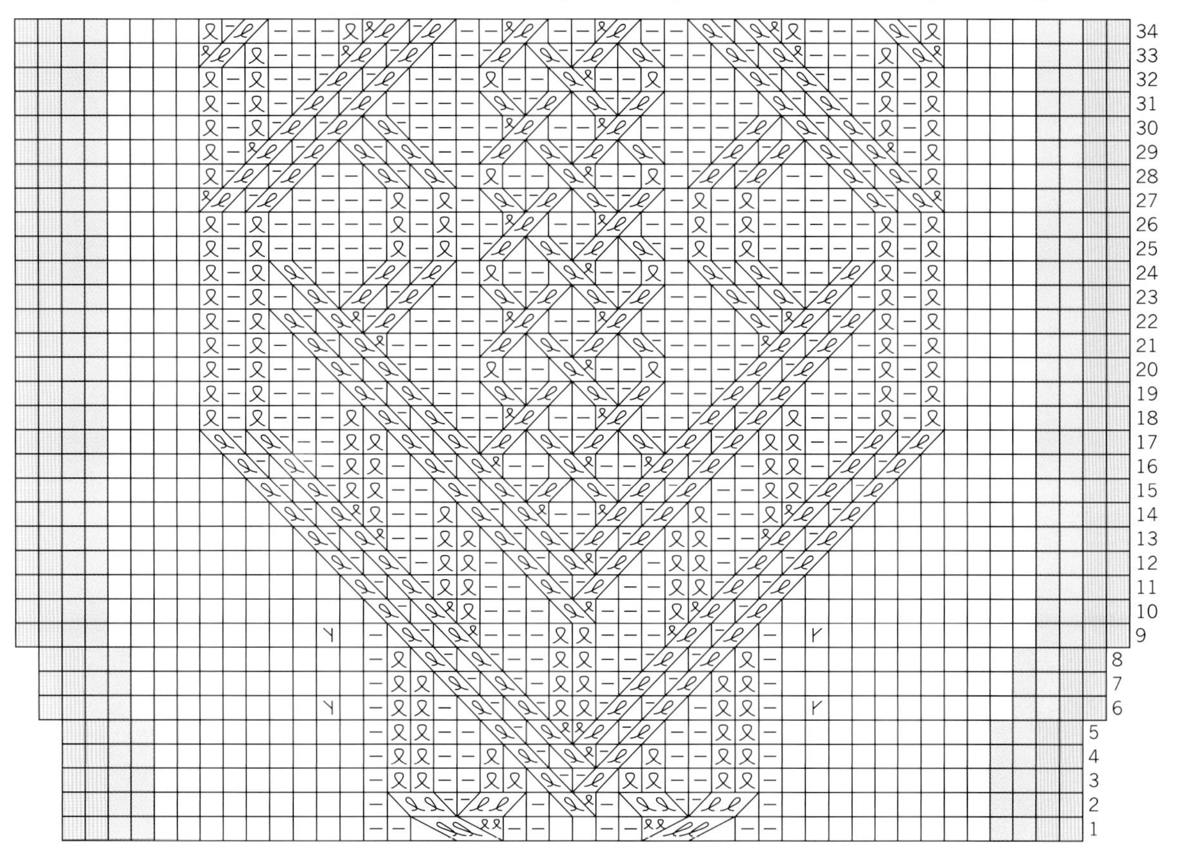

Size L only — Sizes XS, S and M skip these squares

Sizes M and L only — Sizes XS and S skip these squares

Sizes S, M and L only — Size XS skip these squares

C

9 stitches

B

Work 3 [4, 5, 6] times

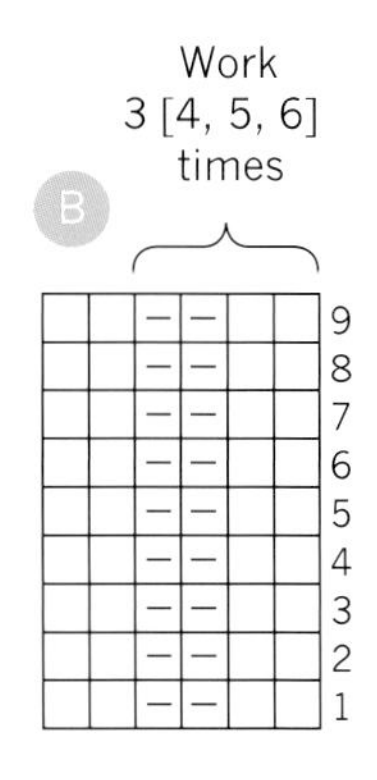

A

9 stitches

G

8 stitches

16
15
14
13
12
11
10
9
8
7
6
5
4
3
2
1

Size L only — Sizes XS, S and M skip these squares

Sizes M and L only — Sizes XS and S skip these squares

Sizes S, M and L only — Size XS skip these squares

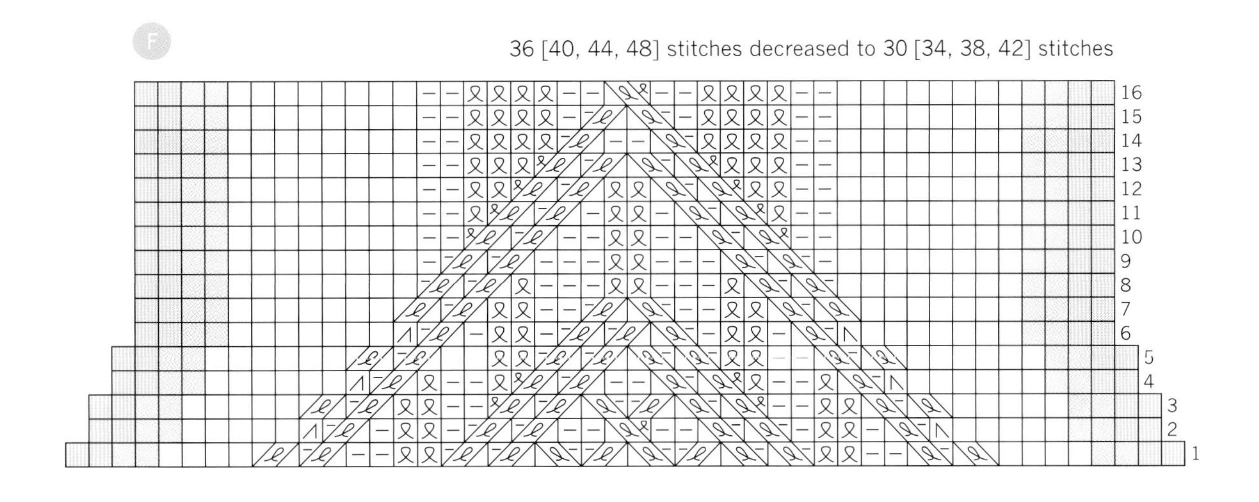

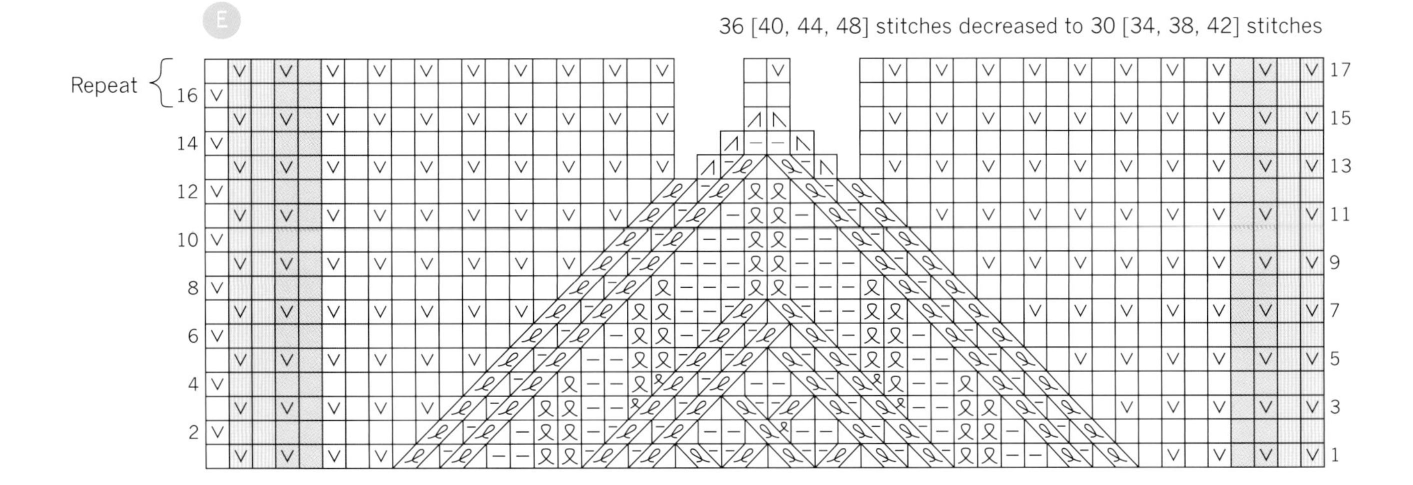

In and Out

Lines of knit zig zag in and out over a background of purls in these playful socks. As a set up for the heel flap, the purl background is replaced with the standard slipped stitch patterning for the heel. As the pattern transitions into the foot, lines begin to straighten out and angle across the top of the foot.

0 NOTES

Left and right socks are mirror images of each other. Directions are the same for both unless otherwise indicated. The diagrams on page 123 outline the differences between the two socks. There are 2 versions of each chart. Charts A, B and C for left and right socks are on page 124 and 126 respectively. Chart D for both socks is on page 127. Make sure to use the appropriate chart for each sock.

1 CUFF

Cast on 66 stitches. Being careful not to twist, join for working in the round and mark beginning of round (page 168). Work chart A for appropriate sock (see Notes in Section 0) for one inch.

2 LEG

Work 2 vertical repeats of chart B for appropriate sock (Left or Right), shifting beginning of round 4 stitches at the end of each vertical repeat as indicated by chart, then work rows 1 through 7 of chart B. Work chart C.

3L HEEL FLAP - LEFT SOCK ONLY

(K1, slip 1 purlwise with yarn in back) 15 times, k2. Divide for heel flap by placing next 33 stitches on hold for top of foot. Heel flap is worked back and forth over remaining 33 stitches—32 stitches just worked plus additional stitch from end of previous round.

Turn work so that wrong side is facing.

SIZES
One size

YARN
Cascade Heritage
75% superwash merino wool /
25% nylon
400 meters per 100g
1 skein of color #5614

NEEDLES
US Size 1 / 2.25mm
or size needed to obtain gauge

NOTIONS
Tapestry needle

GAUGE
In stockinette
32 stitches and 48 rows = 4"

In pattern
32 stitches and 48 rows = 4"

MEASUREMENTS

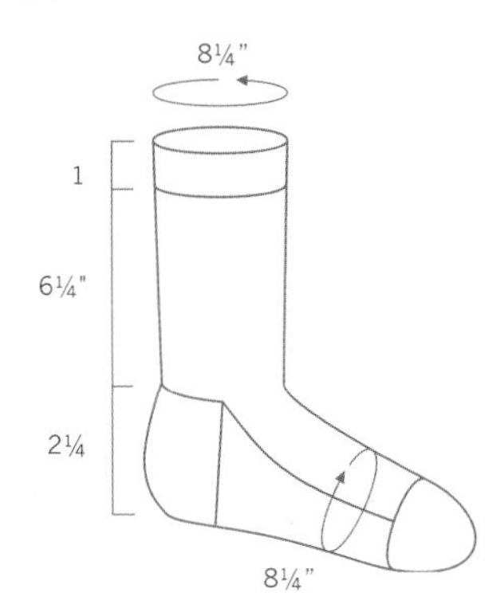

Row 1 (wrong side) Slip 1 purlwise with yarn in front, p32, turn.

Row 2 (right side) (Slip 1 purlwise with yarn in back, k1) 16 times, k1, turn.

Repeat last 2 rows until heel flap measures 2¼ inches, ending ready to work a right side row.

3R HEEL FLAP - RIGHT SOCK ONLY

K1. Divide for heel flap by placing next 33 stitches on hold for top of foot. Heel flap is worked back and forth over remaining 33 stitches—1 stitch just worked plus additional 32 stitches from end of previous round.

Turn work so that wrong side is facing.

Row 1 (wrong side) (Slip 1 purlwise with yarn in front, p1) 16 times, p1, turn.

Row 2 (right side) Slip 1 purlwise with yarn in back, k32, turn.

Repeat last 2 rows until heel flap measures 2¼ inches, ending ready to work a right side row.

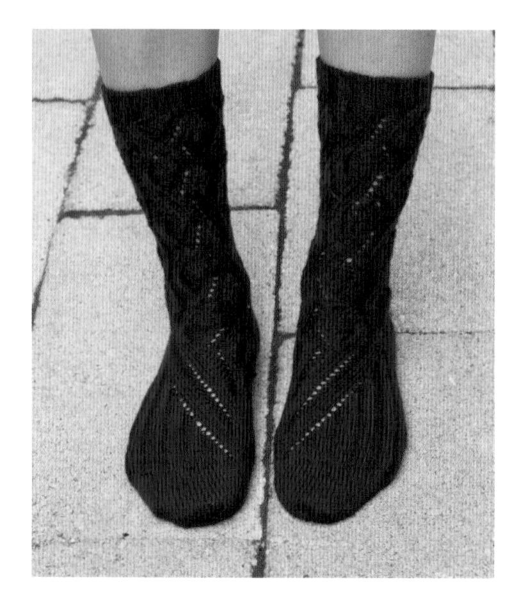

4 TURN HEEL

Continue working back and forth. Use short rows to turn heel as follows:

Row 1 (right side) Slip 1 purlwise with yarn in back, k17, ssk, k1, turn.

Row 2 (wrong side) Slip 1 purlwise with yarn in front, p4, p2tog, p1, turn.

Row 3 Slip 1 purlwise with yarn in back, knit to gap caused by turn on previous row, ssk (using one stitch from each side of gap), k1, turn.

Row 4 Slip 1 purlwise with yarn in front, purl to gap caused by turn on previous row, p2tog (using one stitch from each side of gap), p1, turn.

Repeat last 2 rows until all heel stitches have been worked, ending ready to work a right side row. 19 heel stitches.

5 FOOT

Resume working in the round as follows: Slip 1 purlwise with yarn in back, k8. Mark beginning of round. Knit remaining heel stitches, pick up and knit into each slipped stitch along edge of heel flap, make 1, mark right side of foot, work chart D across held stitches, mark left side of foot, make 1, pick up and knit into each slipped stitch along edge of heel flap, knit to end of round.

Right and left side markers divide foot into top of foot section (previously held stitches) and sole. Decrease 2 sole stitches every other round as follows:

Round 1 Knit to 2 stitches before right side of foot, k2tog, work chart D to left side of foot, ssk, knit to end of round. 2 stitches decreased.

Round 2 Knit to right side of foot, work chart D to left side of foot, knit to end of round.

Repeat last 2 rounds until 66 stitches remain—33 top of foot stitches and 33 sole stitches.

Continue working even, without decreasing sole stitches, until foot measures 2 inches less than desired length from back of heel turn.

6 TOE

Knit to right side of foot. This is the new beginning of round.

Round 1 Knit to end of round.

Round 2 K1, ssk, knit to 3 stitches before left side of foot, k2tog, k2 (one stitch before and one stitch after left side of foot marker), ssk, knit to 3 stitches before right side of foot, k2tog, k1. 4 stitches decreased.

Repeat last 2 rounds until foot measures desired length, ending after a decrease round. Graft top of foot stitches to sole stitches using Kitchener stitch (page 167). Weave in ends and block.

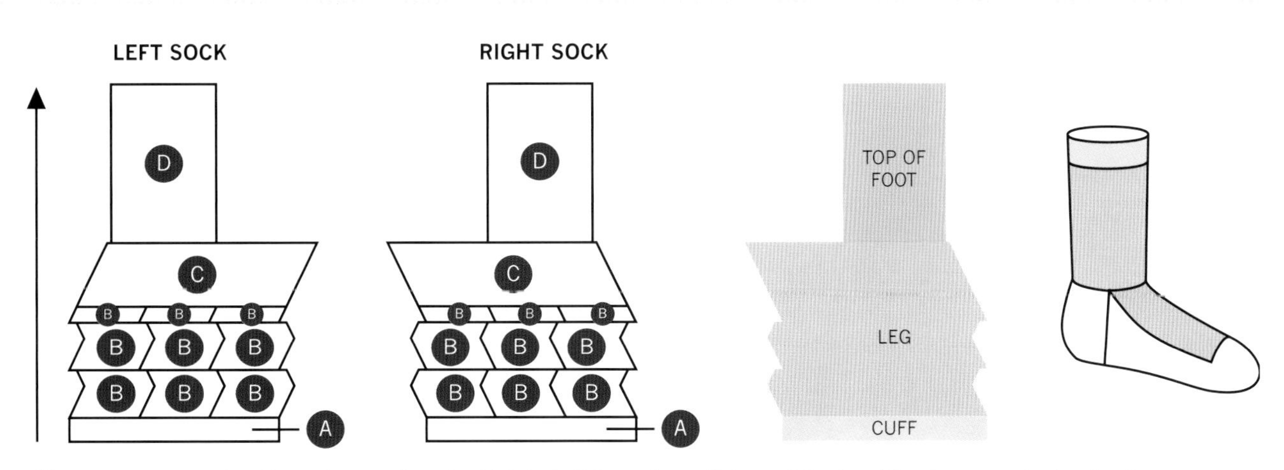

Diagrams represent patterned area of sock which is knit from the cuff toward the toe. Charts are worked as in diagram.

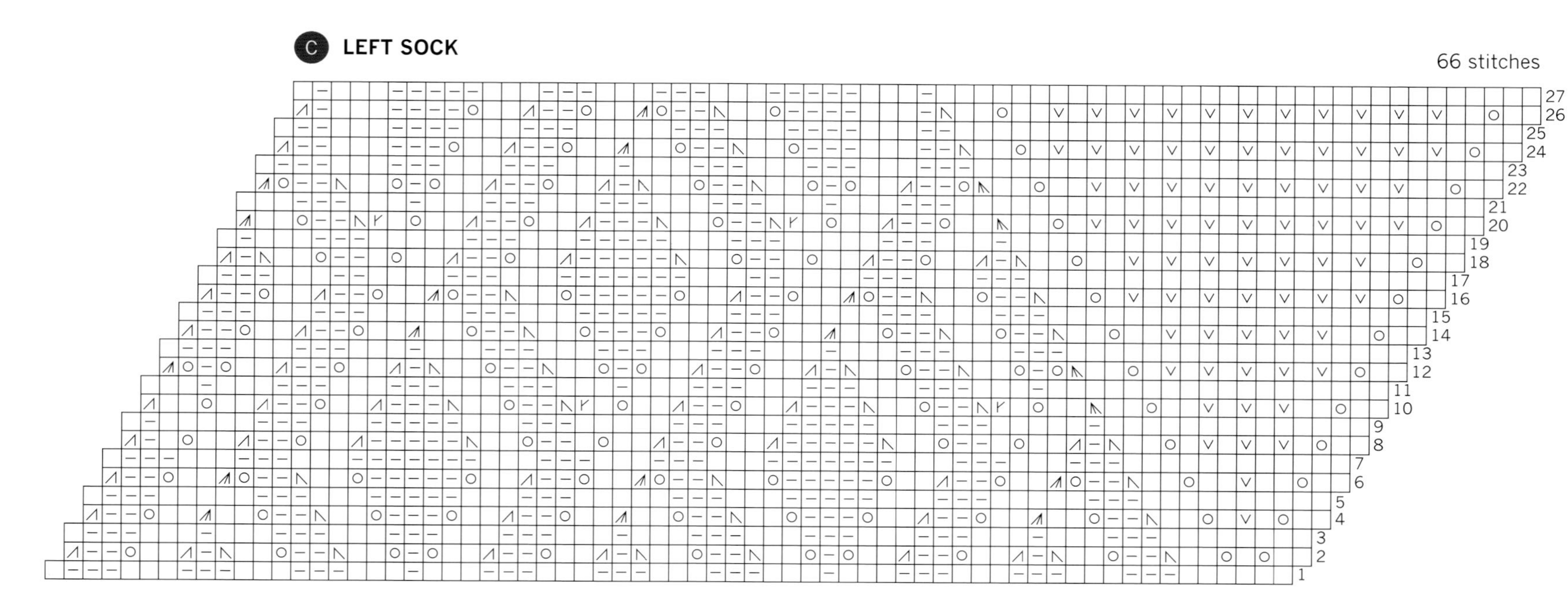

- Knit
- Purl
- Yarnover
- Make 1 left
- Make 1 right
- Slip 1 purlwise with yarn in back
- End Chart B after row 7
- After row 20 of chart B, shift beginning of round 4 stitches to the left as follows: k2, p1, k1, mark new beginning of round.
- K2tog
- Ssk
- K3tog
- Sssk

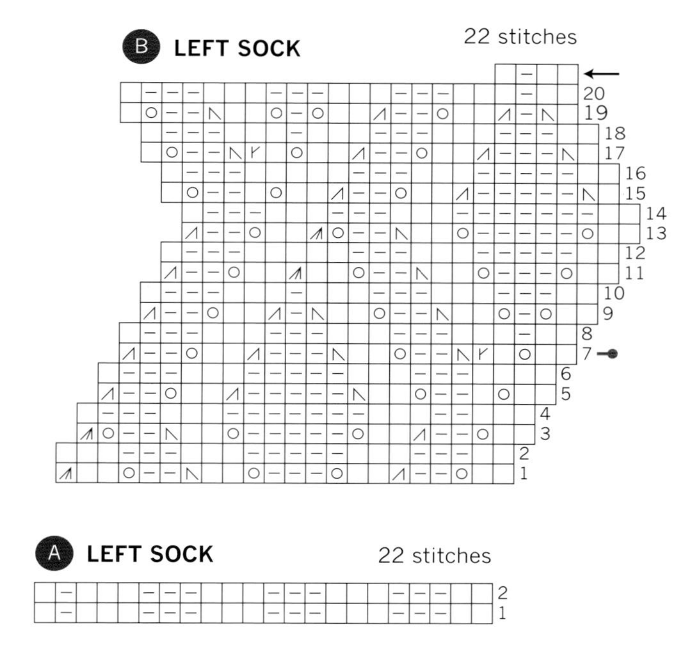

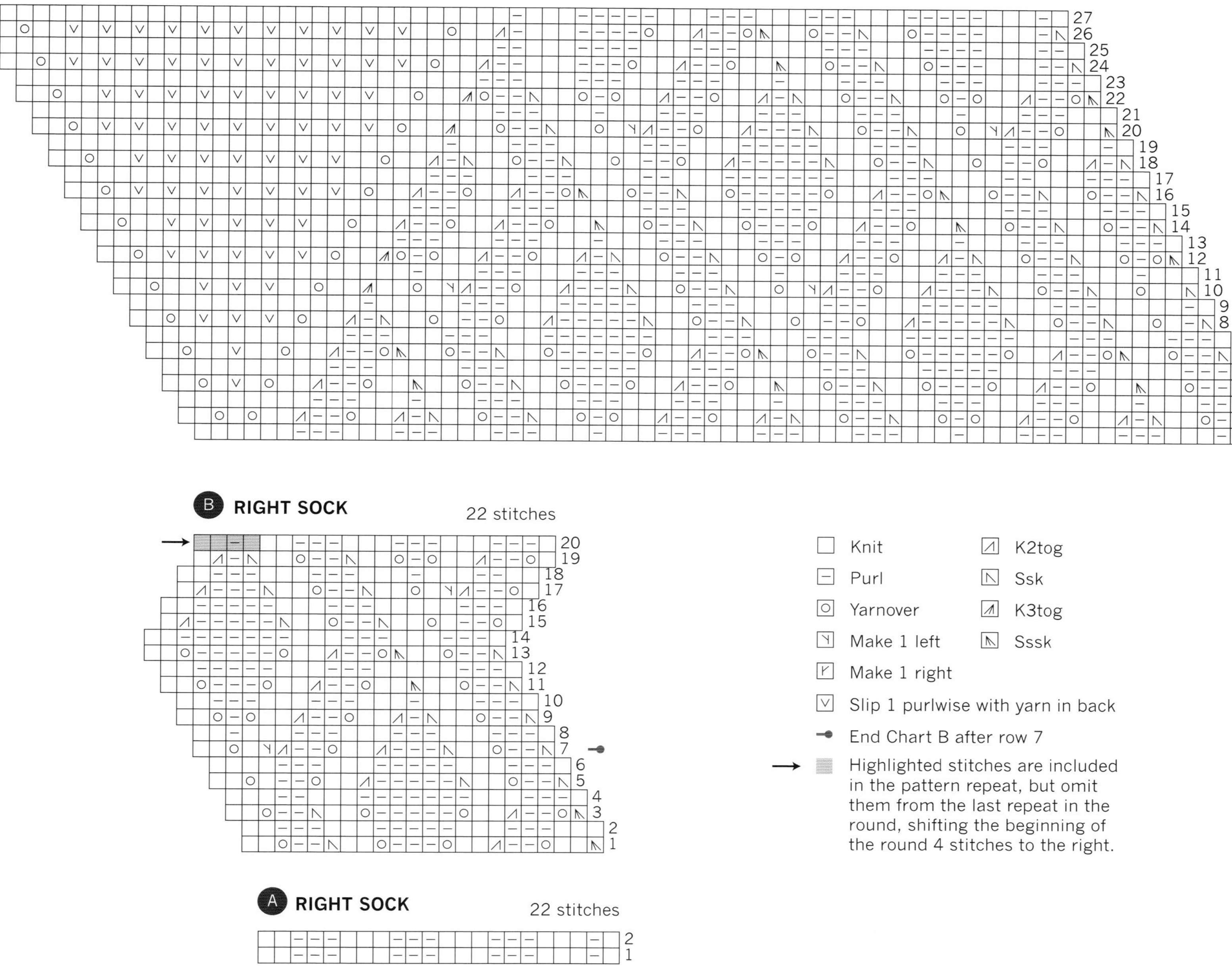

Knit

Purl

Yarnover

Make 1 left

Make 1 right

Slip 1 purlwise with yarn in back

End Chart B after row 7

Highlighted stitches are included in the pattern repeat, but omit them from the last repeat in the round, shifting the beginning of the round 4 stitches to the right.

K2tog

Ssk

K3tog

Sssk

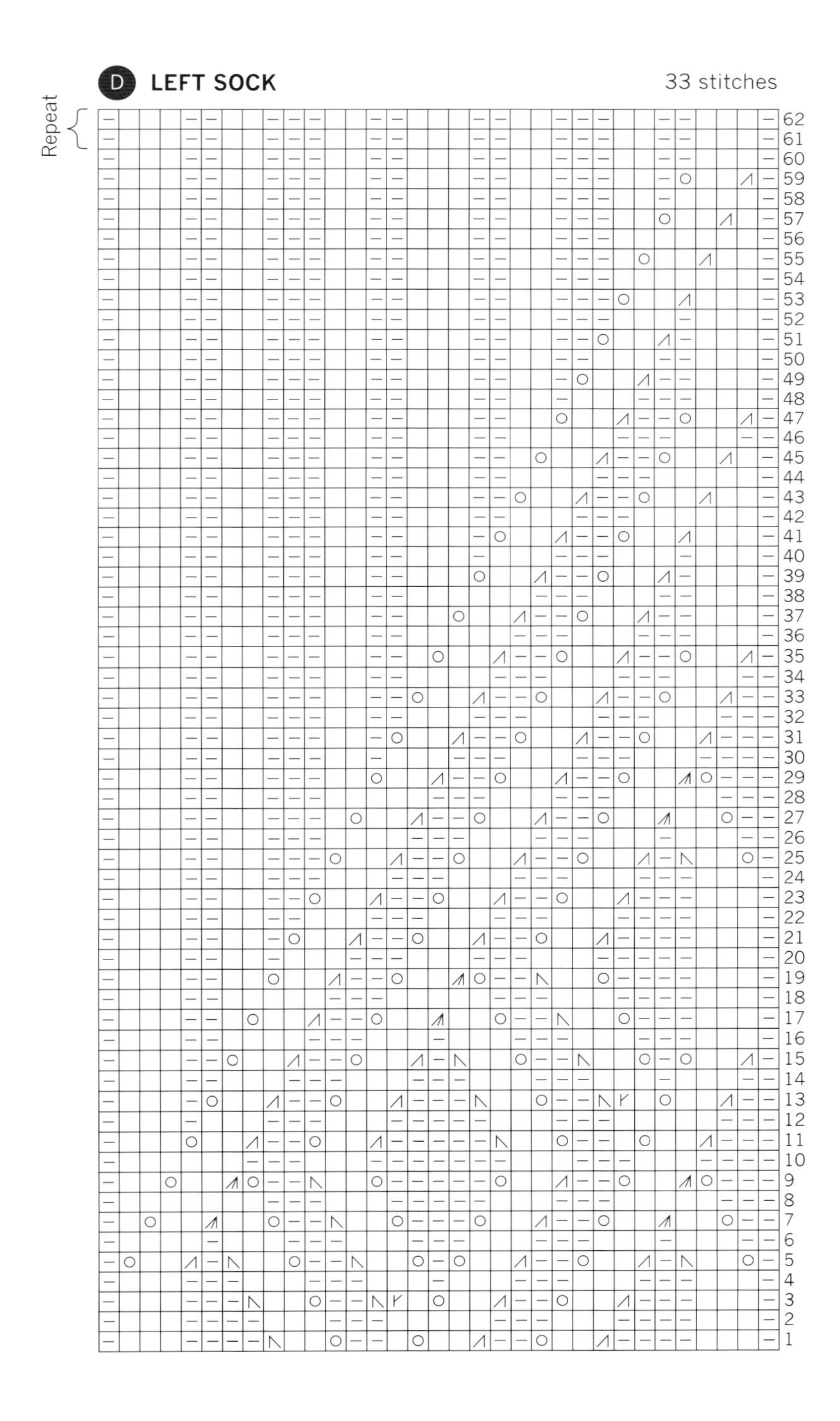
D LEFT SOCK
33 stitches
Repeat

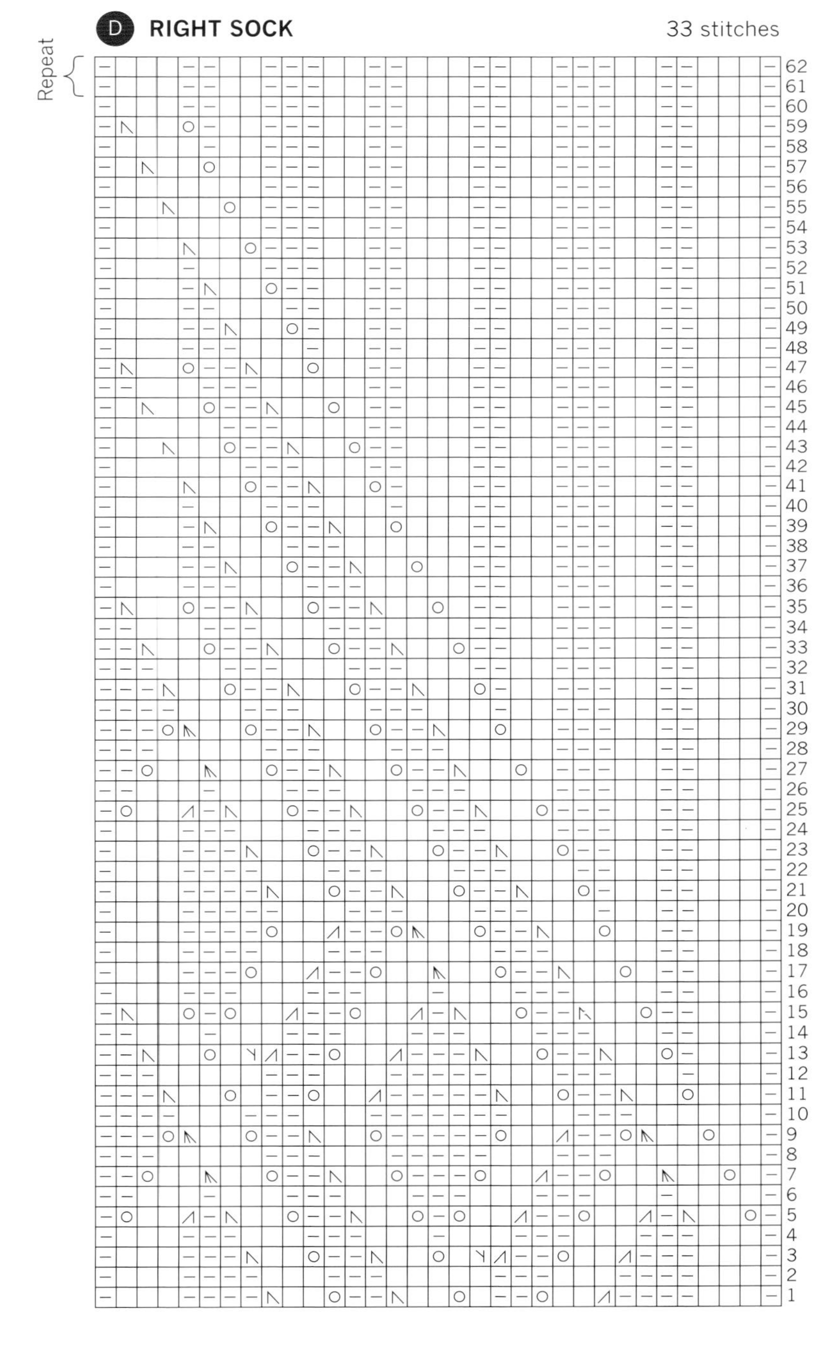
D RIGHT SOCK
33 stitches
Repeat

Cusp

Diagonal lines loop around from the back of the sock to the top of the foot creating cusp points at both locations. Lace diamonds tessellate the space between the lines. Vertical twisted rib on the leg contrasts the diagonal lace lines while unusual gusset shaping follows the lace patterning on top of the foot, drawing the gusset ribbing in parallel to the diagonal lines.

1 CUFF

Cast on 65 [73] stitches for working in the round. Being careful not to twist, join for working in the round and mark beginning of round (page 168). Work chart A (page 134), repeating marked section as indicated, for one inch.

2 LEG - CHART B

Begin working chart B as follows.

Round 1 (patterned round) Work lace section 1 (see diagram on page 135) of chart B, place marker, ssk, work stitches as set (see sidebar on page 130) to last 2 stitches of round, k2tog. 64 [72] stitches.

Round 2 (set round) Knit to marker, k1, work stitches as set to last stitch of round, k1.

Continue working as established, alternating patterned and set rounds, through row 17 of chart B. Work one set round. Shift beginning of round 1 stitch to the left by knitting 1 stitch and marking new beginning of round.

Round 19 (patterned round) Work lace section 1 of chart B, ssk, work stitches as set to 3 stitches before end of round, k2tog, place marker for lace section 2 of chart B, work lace section 2 of chart B to end of round.

Round 20 (set round) Knit to marker, k1, work stitches as set to 1 stitch before marker, k1, knit to end of round.

Continue working in established pattern, alternating patterned and set rounds, through row 33 of chart B. Work one set round.

SIZES
S [L] — shown in size S

YARN
Cascade Heritage
75% superwash merino wool /
25% nylon
400 meters per 100g
1 skein of color #5616

NEEDLES
US Size 1 / 2.25mm
or size needed to obtain gauge

NOTIONS
Stitch markers, tapestry needle

GAUGE
In stockinette
32 stitches and 48 rows = 4"

In pattern
32 stitches and 48 rows = 4"

MEASUREMENTS

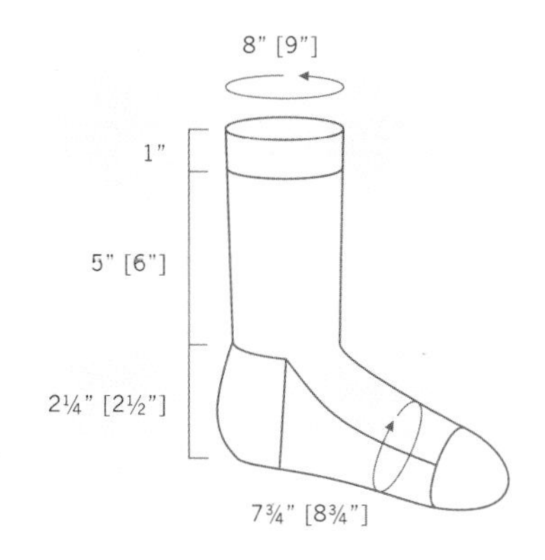

Round 35 Work lace section 1 of chart B, ssk, work stitches as set to 2 stitches before marker, k2tog, work lace section 2 of chart B, place marker, yo, k1, yo.

Round 36 Knit to marker, k1, work stitches as set to 1 stitch before marker, k1, knit to marker, p1, k1 tbl, p1.

Round 37 (patterned round) Work lace section 1 of chart B, ssk, work stitches as set to 2 stitches before marker, k2tog, work lace section 2 of chart B, yo, work stitches in rib (see sidebar) to end of round, yo before end of round.

Round 38 (set round) Knit to marker, k1, work stitches as set to 1 stitch before marker, k1, knit to marker, work stitches in rib to end of round.

Begin working 8-row repeat section, continuing in established pattern, alternating patterned and set rounds, until 3 stitches remain between lace section 1 and 2, ending with a patterned round.

Work lace section 3 of chart B as follows:

Set-up for section 3 Knit to marker, remove marker, k1, k1 tbl, k1, remove marker, knit to marker, remove marker, work stitches in rib to end of round.

Round 1 Work lace section 3 of chart B, work stitches in rib to end of round.

WORK STITCHES AS SET

On the right side
Knit the knits. Purl the purls. Knit tbl the knit tbl's.

On the wrong side
Knit the knits and purl tbl all other stitches.

WORK STITCHES IN RIB

Knit tbl the knits and knit tbls. Purl the purls. To work a yarnover in rib after a marker, knit it if the third stitch on the left needle is a knit tbl, otherwise purl it. To work a yarnover in rib before a marker, knit it if the third to last stitch worked was a knit tbl, otherwise purl it.

3 HEEL FLAP

Divide for heel flap by placing next 35 stitches on hold for top of foot. Heel flap is worked back and forth over remaining 29 [37] stitches. Turn work so that wrong side is facing.

Row 1 (wrong side) Slip 1 purlwise with yarn in front, work 27 [35] stitches as set (see sidebar), p1, turn.

Row 2 (right side) Slip 1 purlwise with yarn in back, work 27 [35] stitches as set, k1, turn.

Repeat last 2 rows until heel flap measures 2¼ [2½] inches, ending ready to work a right side row.

4 TURN HEEL

Continue working back and forth. Use short rows to turn heel as follows:

Row 1 (right side) Slip 1 purlwise with yarn in back, k15 [19], ssk, k1, turn.

Row 2 (wrong side) Slip 1 purlwise with yarn in front, p4, p2tog, p1, turn

Row 3 Slip 1 purlwise with yarn in back, knit to one stitch before gap caused by turn on previous row, ssk (using one stitch from each side of gap), k1, turn.

Row 4 Slip 1 purlwise with yarn in front, purl to one stitch before gap caused by turn on previous row, p2tog (using one stitch from each side of gap), p1, turn.

Repeat last 2 rows until all heel stitches have been worked, ending ready to work a right side row. 17 [21] heel stitches.

5 SHAPE GUSSETS

Resume working in the round as follows: Slip 1 purlwise with yarn in back, k8 [10]. Mark beginning of round. Knit remaining heel stitches, pick up and knit into each slipped stitch along edge of heel flap, mark right side of foot, make 1, knit across held stitches, make 1, mark left side of foot, pick up and knit into each slipped stitch along edge of heel flap, knit to end of round.

Round 1 (patterned round) Knit to 14 [17] stitches before right side of foot, place marker, p2, (k1 tbl, p2) to marker, work chart C across top of foot, (p2, k1 tbl) 4 [5] times, p2, place marker, knit to end of round. 2 stitches decreased.

Round 2 (set round) Knit to marker, work stitches as set to marker, knit to marker, work stitches as set to marker, knit to end of round.

Continue in established pattern, alternating patterned and set rounds, decreasing 2 stitches in chart C section every patterned round until 62 [70] stitches remain, ending after a set round.

6 FOOT

Continue decreasing within chart C, but introduce 2 increases per patterned round to maintain stitch count as follows:

Next round (patterned round) Knit to 1 stitch before marker, make 1 right, k1, work stitches as set to marker, work chart C to marker, work stitches as set to marker, k1, make 1 left, knit to end of round.

Next round (set round) Knit to marker, work stitches as set to marker, knit to marker, work stitches as set to marker, knit to end of round.

Repeat last 2 rounds through end of chart C.

Next round Knit to marker (this is now the right side of foot marker), work stitches as set to marker, remove marker, k1 tbl, remove marker, work stitches as set to marker (this is now the left side of foot marker), knit to end of round. 62 [70] stitches—29 [35] top of foot stitches and 33 [35] sole stitches.

Next round Knit to marker, work stitches as set across top of foot, knit to end of round.

Continue working all stitches as set until foot measures 2 inches less than desired length from back of heel turn.

7 TOE

Size S only Shift one stitch from either side of sole to top of foot so that top of foot and sole each have 31 stitches.

Both sizes Knit to right side of foot. This is the new beginning of round.

Round 1 Knit to end of round.

Round 2 K1, ssk, knit to 3 stitches before left side of foot, k2tog, k2 (one stitch before and one stitch after left side of foot marker), ssk, knit to 3 stitches before right side of foot, k2tog, k1. 4 stitches decreased.

Repeat last 2 rounds until foot measures desired length, ending after a decrease round. Graft top of foot stitches to sole stitches using Kitchener stitch (page 167). Weave in ends and block.

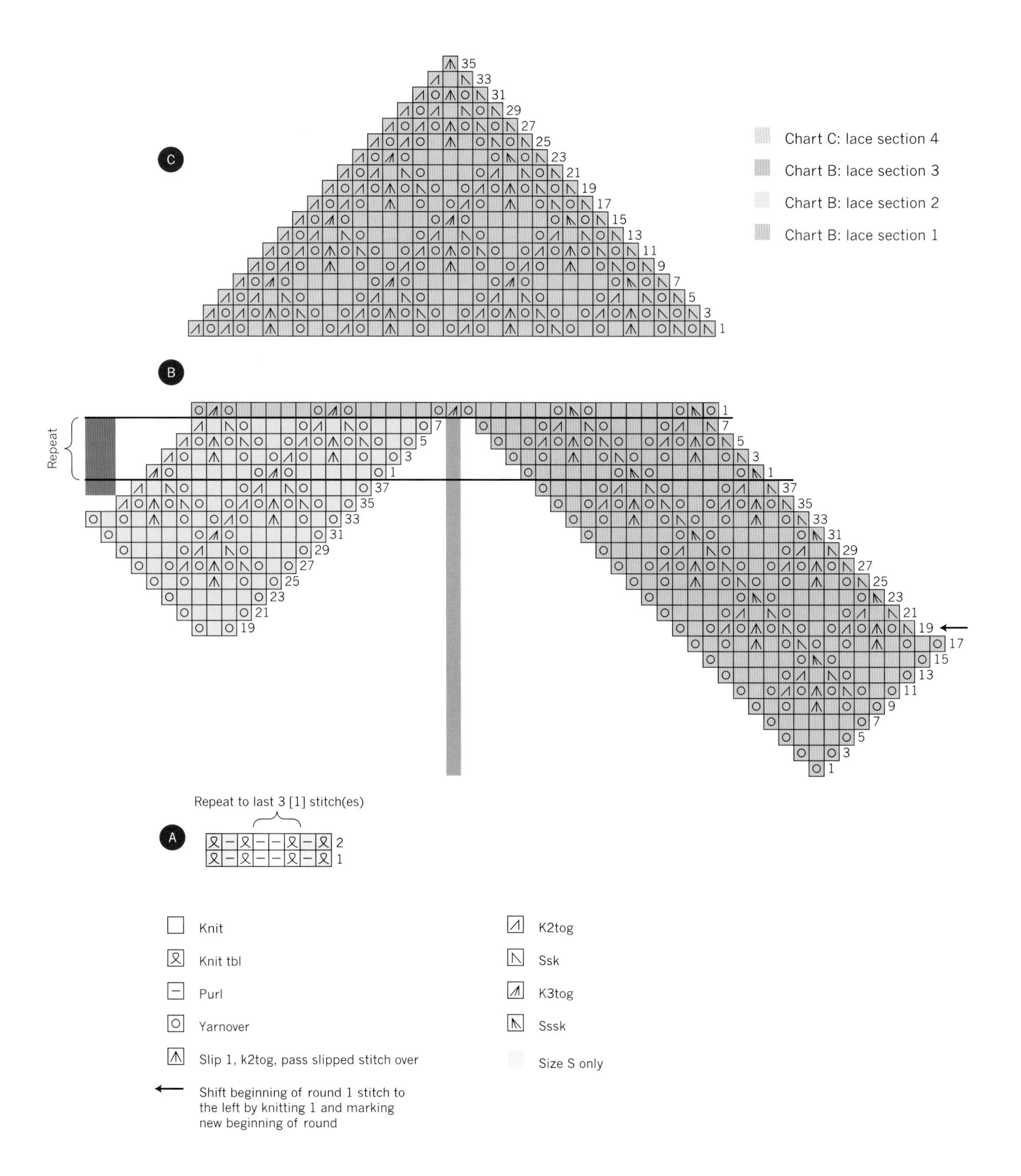

C
Chart C: lace section 4
Chart B: lace section 3
Chart B: lace section 2
Chart B: lace section 1
B
Repeat
A
Repeat to last 3 [1] stitch(es)
Knit
Knit tbl
Purl
Yarnover
Slip 1, k2tog, pass slipped stitch over
Shift beginning of round 1 stitch to the left by knitting 1 and marking new beginning of round
K2tog
Ssk
K3tog
Sssk
Size S only

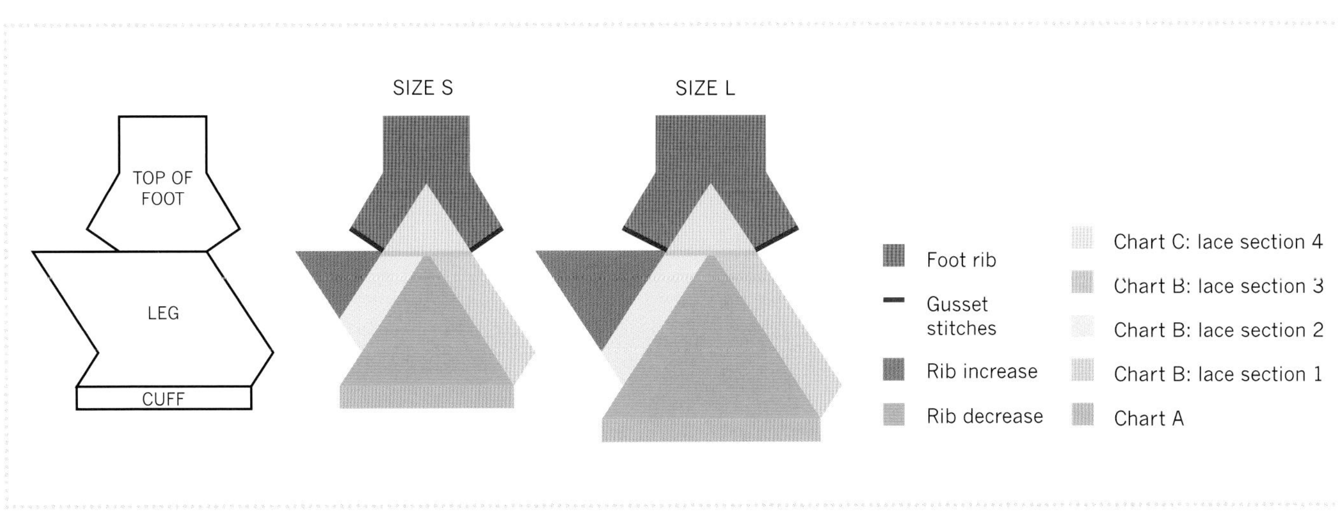

TOP OF FOOT
LEG
CUFF
SIZE S
SIZE L
Foot rib
Gusset stitches
Rib increase
Rib decrease
Chart C: lace section 4
Chart B: lace section 3
Chart B: lace section 2
Chart B: lace section 1
Chart A

Pointelle

In this pattern, the diagonal lines are kept simple while the background is more textured. Simple yarnover eyelets emanate from an arrowhead lace pattern and swirl across the leg in one direction and then in the opposite. The same arrowhead lace grows throughout the sock as the diagonal line cuts across the top of the foot. Right and left socks are mirror images.

0 NOTES

Left and right socks are mirror images of each other. Directions are the same for both unless otherwise indicated. The diagrams on pages 142 and 144 outline the differences between the right and left sock respectively. The right sock uses charts A, B, C and D on pages 142 and 143. The left sock uses charts E, F, G and H on pages 144 and 145.

1 CUFF

Cast on 60 [70] stitches. Being careful not to twist, join for working in the round and mark beginning of round (page 168).

Right Sock Work chart A for one inch.

Left Sock Work chart E for one inch.

2 LEG

Right Sock Work chart B, then chart C, ending with row 68 [78] of chart C. Note that odd rounds are not charted. Knit all stitches for odd rounds. On round 22 of chart B, shift beginning of round 2 stitches to the left as follows: K2, mark new beginning of round, work round 22 as charted.

Left Sock Work chart F, then chart G, ending with row 68 [78] of chart G. Note that odd rounds are not charted. Knit all stitches for odd rounds. On round 21 of chart F, shift beginning of round 2 stitches to the right as follows: Knit to 2 stitches before the end of round, mark new beginning of round and proceed to round 22.

SIZES
S [L] — shown in size S

YARN
Version 1 Fortissima Socka
75% wool / 25% nylon
231 yards per 50g
2 skeins of Orangello #1007

Version 2 Blue Moon Fiber Arts
Socks That Rock Lightweight
100% superwash merino wool
360 yards per 4.5 oz
1 [2] skeins of Jasper (Purple)

NEEDLES
US Size 1 / 2.25mm
or size needed to obtain gauge

NOTIONS
Tapestry needle

GAUGE
In stockinette
32 stitches and 48 rows = 4"

In pattern
32 stitches and 48 rows = 4"

MEASUREMENTS

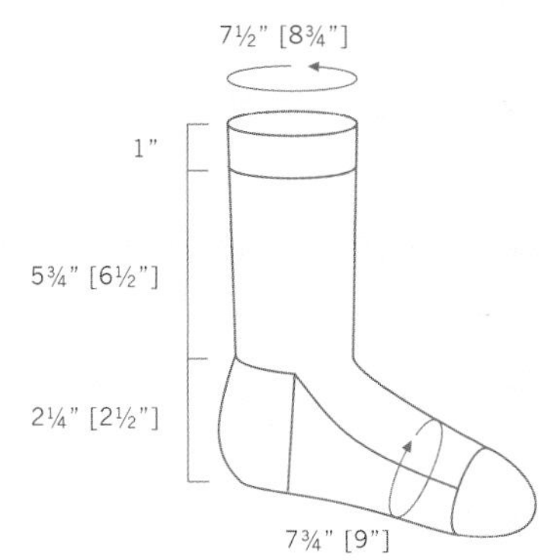

3 HEEL FLAP

Right sock only Knit 28 [33].

Both socks Divide for heel flap by placing next 32 [37] stitches on hold for top of foot. Heel flap is worked back and forth over remaining 28 [33] stitches. Turn work so that wrong side is facing.

Row 1 (wrong side) Slip 1 purlwise with yarn in front, p27 [32], turn.

Row 2 (right side) (Slip 1 purlwise with yarn in back, k1) 14 [16] times, k0 [1], turn.

Repeat last 2 rows until heel flap measures 2¼ [2½] inches, ending ready to work a right side row.

4 TURN HEEL

Continue working back and forth. Use short rows to turn heel as follows:

Row 1 (right side) Slip 1 purlwise with yarn in back, k16 [17], ssk, k1, turn.

Row 2 (wrong side) Slip 1 purlwise with yarn in front, p7 [4], p2tog, p1, turn.

Row 3 Slip 1 purlwise with yarn in back, knit to one stitch before gap caused by turn on previous row, ssk (using one stitch from each side of gap), k1, turn.

Row 4 Slip 1 purlwise with yarn in front, purl to one stitch before gap caused by turn on previous row, p2tog (using one stitch from each side of gap), p1, turn.

Repeat last 2 rows until all heel stitches have been worked, ending ready to work a right side row. 18 [19] heel stitches.

5 FOOT

Resume working in the round as follows: Slip 1 purlwise with yarn in back, k8 [9]. Mark beginning of round. Knit remaining heel stitches, pick up and knit into each slipped stitch along edge of heel flap, make 1, mark right side of foot, knit held stitches, mark left side of foot, make 1, pick up and knit into each slipped stitch along edge of heel flap, knit to end of round.

Right and left side markers divide foot into top of foot section (previously held stitches) and sole. Decrease 2 sole stitches every other round as follows:

Round 2 Knit to 2 stitches before right side of foot, k2tog, work chart D or H (beginning with row 2 of charts) for right or left sock respectively to left side of foot, ssk, knit to end of round. 3 stitches decreased—1 across top of foot and 2 along sole.

Round 3 (plain round) Knit to end of round.

Round 4 (decrease round) Knit to 2 stitches before right side of foot, k2tog, work chart D or H for right or left sock respectively to left side of foot, ssk, knit to end of round. 2 stitches decreased.

Repeat last 2 rounds, alternating plain and decrease rounds until 63 [73] stitches remain—31 [36] top of foot stitches and 32 [37] sole stitches.

Work one more decrease round, except do not work ssk on sole. 62 [72] stitches.

Continue working even, without decreasing sole stitches, by alternating plain and charted rounds on top of foot until foot measures 2 inches less than desired length from back of heel turn.

6 TOE

Knit to right side of foot. This is the new beginning of round.

Round 1 Knit to end of round.

Round 2 K1, ssk, knit to 3 stitches before left side of foot, k2tog, k2 (one stitch before and one stitch after left side of foot marker), ssk, knit to 3 stitches before right side of foot, k2tog, k1. 4 stitches decreased.

Repeat last 2 rounds until foot measures desired length, ending after a decrease round. Graft top of foot stitches to sole stitches using Kitchener stitch (page 167). Weave in ends and block.

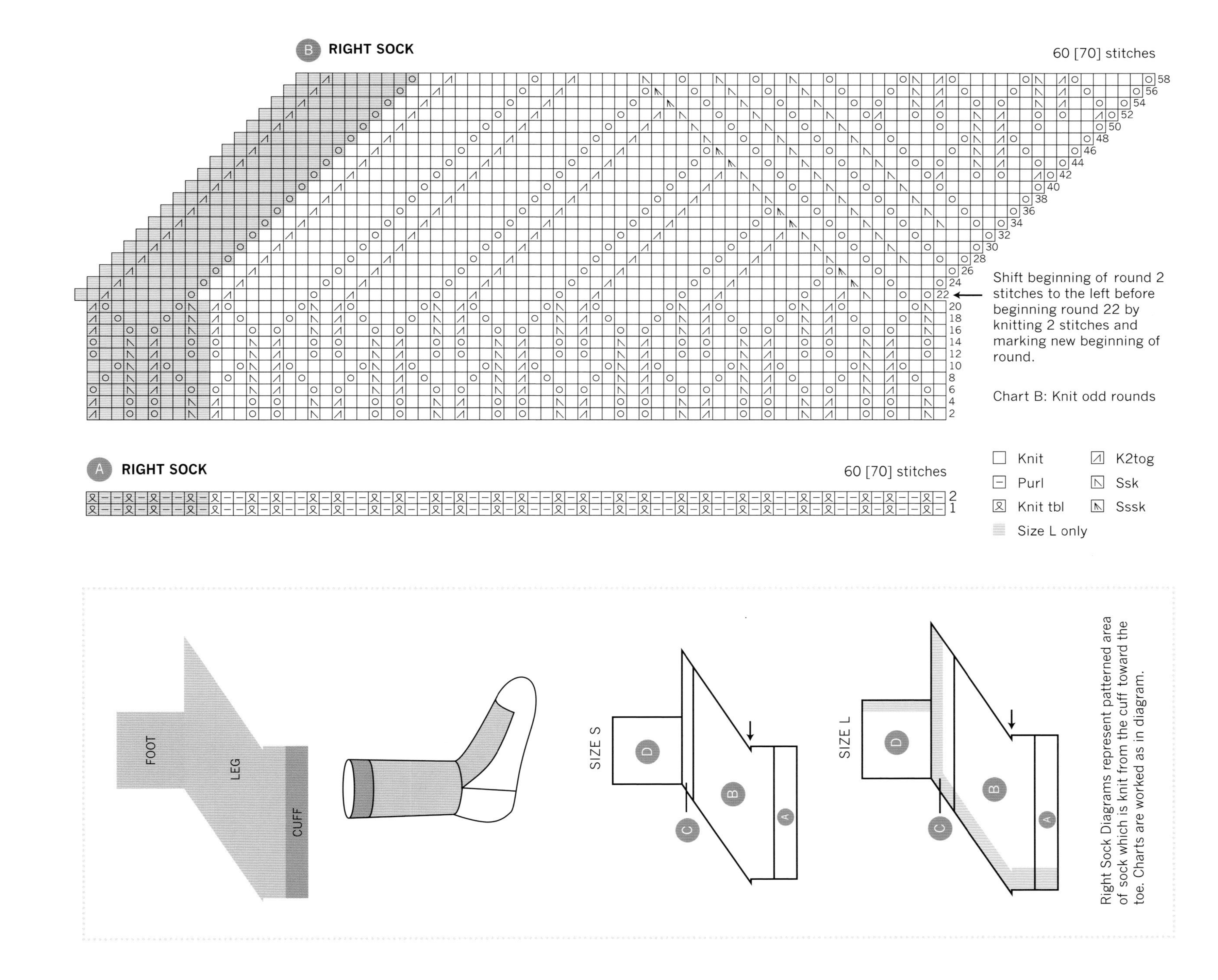

Right Sock Diagrams represent patterned area of sock which is knit from the cuff toward the toe. Charts are worked as in diagram.

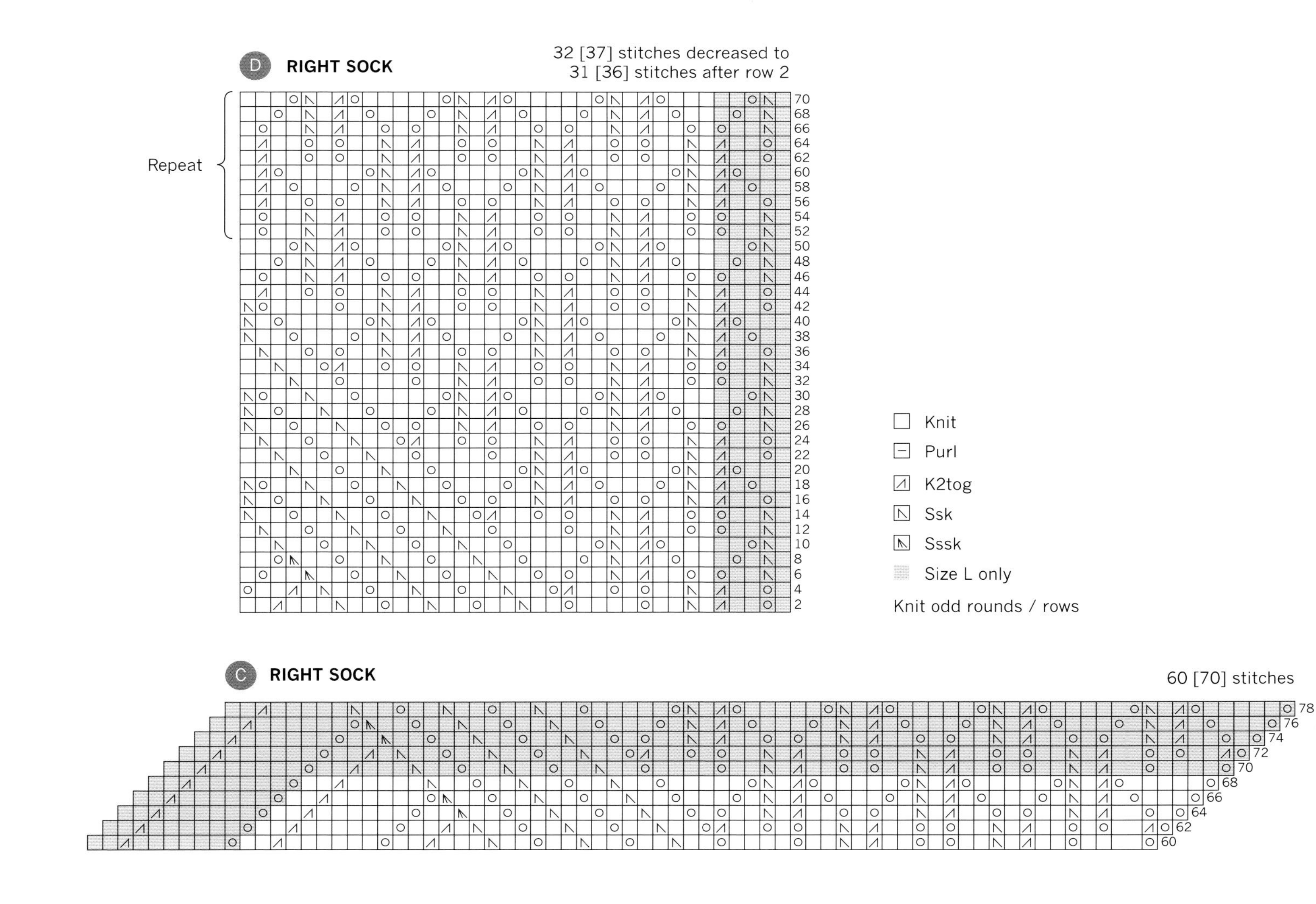
D
RIGHT SOCK
32 [37] stitches decreased to
31 [36] stitches after row 2
Repeat
Knit
Purl
K2tog
Ssk
Sssk
Size L only
Knit odd rounds / rows
C
RIGHT SOCK
60 [70] stitches

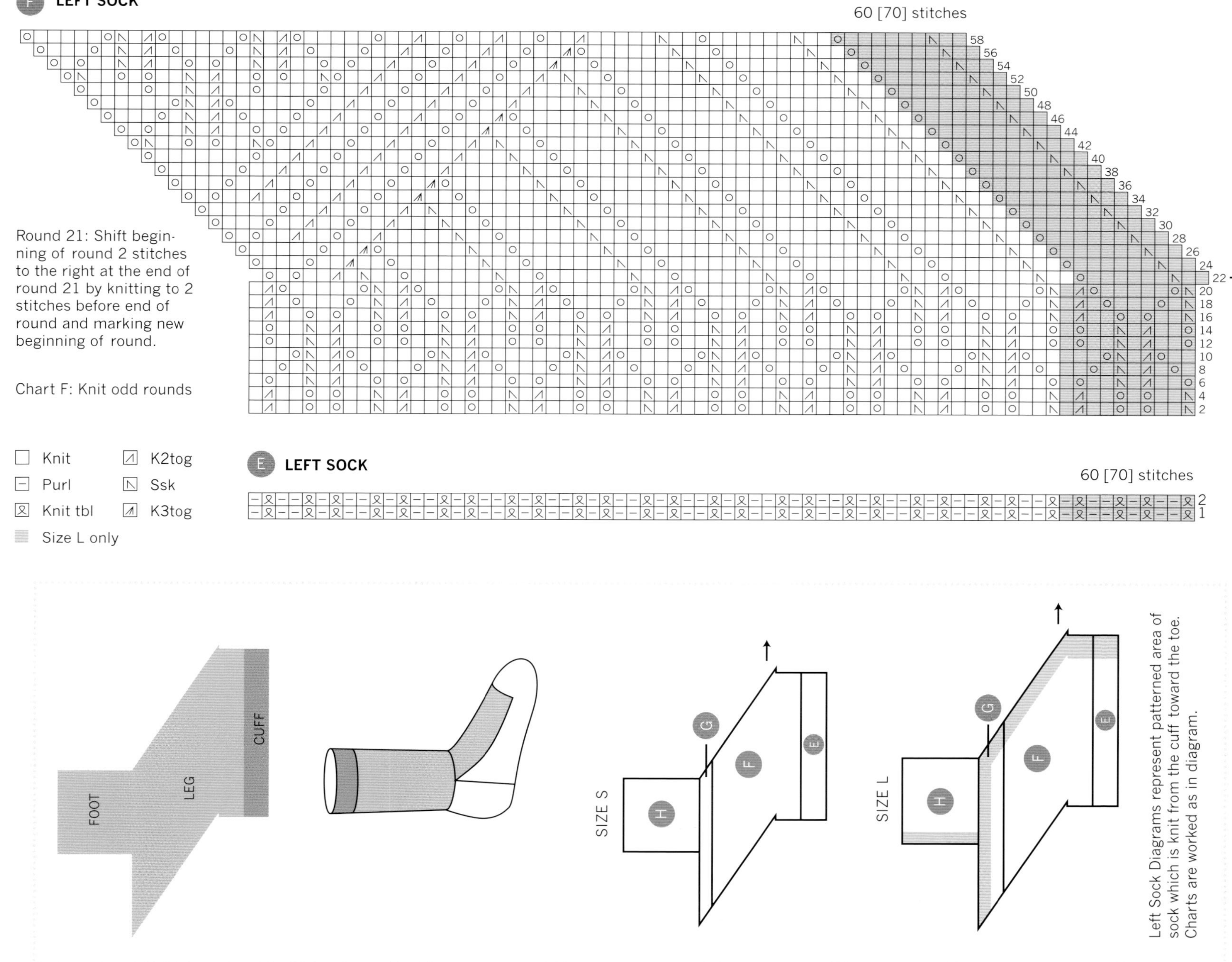

Left Sock Diagrams represent patterned area of sock which is knit from the cuff toward the toe. Charts are worked as in diagram.

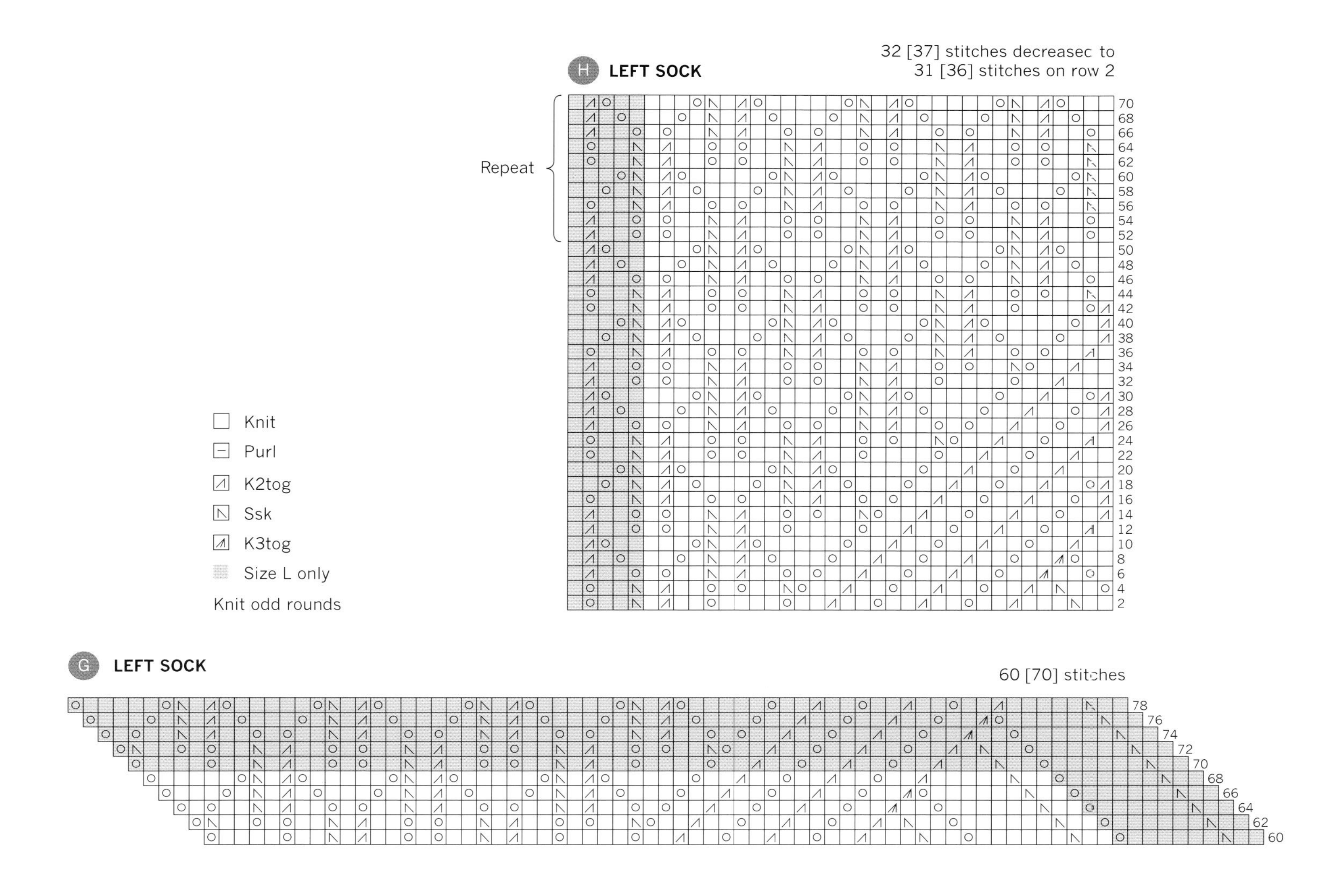
H LEFT SOCK
32 [37] stitches decreased to
31 [36] stitches on row 2
Repeat
Knit
Purl
K2tog
Ssk
K3tog
Size L only
Knit odd rounds
G LEFT SOCK
60 [70] stitches

Sake

One of my favorite foods is sake sashimi, or fresh slices of raw salmon. In these namesake socks, cables angle in and out to form diagonal lines reminiscent of the beautiful striations of fat in salmon—the fat is what makes it taste good! For added fun, sake is also rice wine (pronounced differently, I am told). I don't recommend drinking and knitting though—at least not this sock!

1 LEG

Cast on 64 stitches. Being careful not to twist, join for working in the round and mark beginning of round (page 168). Work chart A (page 150). 80 stitches.

2 HEEL FLAP

Divide for heel flap by placing previous 40 stitches on hold for top of foot. Work chart B (page 151) back and forth across next 40 stitches for heel flap. 34 heel stitches. Repeat last 2 rows of chart B until heel flap measures 2½ inches, ending ready to work a right side row.

3 TURN HEEL

Continue working back and forth. Use short rows to turn heel as follows:

Row 1 (right side) Slip 1 purlwise with yarn in back, k18, ssk, k1, turn.

Row 2 (wrong side) Slip 1 purlwise with yarn in front, p5, p2tog, p1, turn.

Row 3 Slip 1 purlwise with yarn in back, knit to one stitch before gap caused by turn on previous row, ssk (using one stitch from each side of gap), k1, turn.

Row 4 Slip 1 purlwise with yarn in front, purl to one stitch before gap caused by turn on previous row, p2tog (using one stitch from each side of gap), p1, turn.

Repeat last 2 rows until all heel stitches have been worked, ending ready to work a right side row. 20 heel stitches.

SIZES
One size

YARN
Shelridge Farm Soft Touch Ultra
100% wool
185 yards per 50g
2 skeins of Pumpkin

NEEDLES
US Size 1 / 2.25mm
or size needed to obtain gauge

NOTIONS
Cable needle, tapestry needle

GAUGE
In stockinette
32 stitches and 48 rows = 4"

In pattern
40 stitches and 48 rows = 4"

MEASUREMENTS

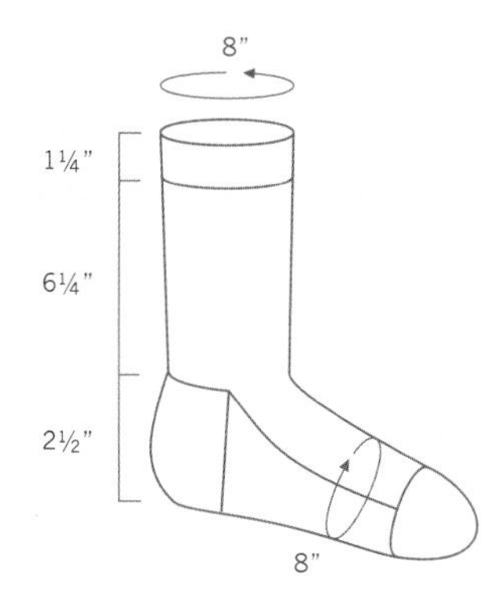

4 FOOT

Resume working in the round as follows: Slip 1 purlwise with yarn in back, k9. Mark beginning of round. Knit remaining heel stitches, pick up and knit into each slipped stitch along edge of heel flap, make 1, mark right side of foot, work chart C (page 152) across held stitches, mark left side of foot, make 1, pick up and knit into each slipped stitch along edge of heel flap, knit to end of round.

Right and left side markers divide foot into top of foot section (previously held stitches) and sole. Decrease 2 sole stitches every other round as follows:

Round 1 Knit to 2 stitches before right side of foot, k2tog, work chart C to left side of foot, ssk, knit to end of round. 2 stitches decreased.

Round 2 Knit to right side of foot, work chart C to left side of foot, knit to end of round.

Repeat last 2 rounds until 72 stitches remain—40 top of foot stitches and 32 sole stitches.

Continue working even, without decreasing sole stitches, until foot measures as close to, but not longer than, 4 inches less than desired length from back of heel turn, ending after row 38 or 56 of chart C.

If last row of chart C was row 38, then continue working even while working chart D1 (page 153) across top of foot. If last row of chart C was row 56, then continue working even while working chart D2 (page 153) across top of foot. 64 stitches.

Continue in established pattern until foot measures 2 inches less than desired length from back of heel turn.

5 TOE

Knit to right side of foot. This is the new beginning of round.

Round 1 Knit to end of round.

Round 2 K1, ssk, knit to 3 stitches before left side of foot, k2tog, k2 (one stitch before and one stitch after left side of foot marker), ssk, knit to 3 stitches before right side of foot, k2tog, k1. 4 stitches decreased.

Repeat last 2 rounds until foot measures desired length, ending after a decrease round. Graft top of foot stitches to sole stitches using Kitchener stitch (page 167). Weave in ends and block.

64 stitches increased to 80 stitches

Note Beginning of round shifts at the end of rounds 14, 52, 53, 89, and 90. On rounds 14, 53 and 90, two additional stitches are worked at the end of the round, shifting the beginning of round to the left. On rounds 52 and 89, two stitches are omitted from the end of the round, shifting the beginning of the round to the right.

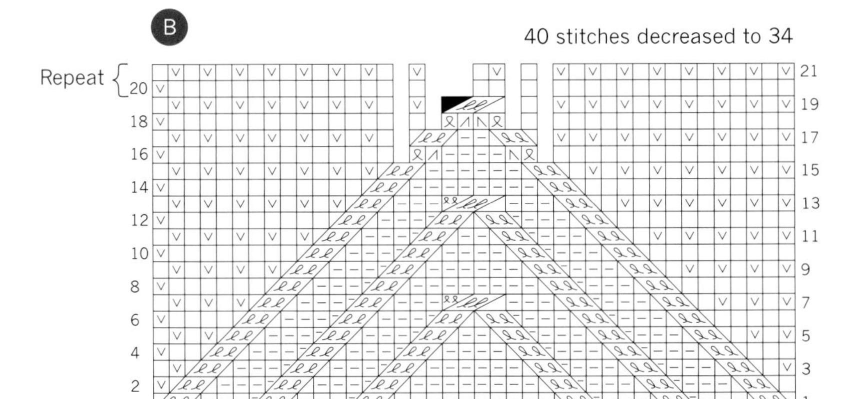

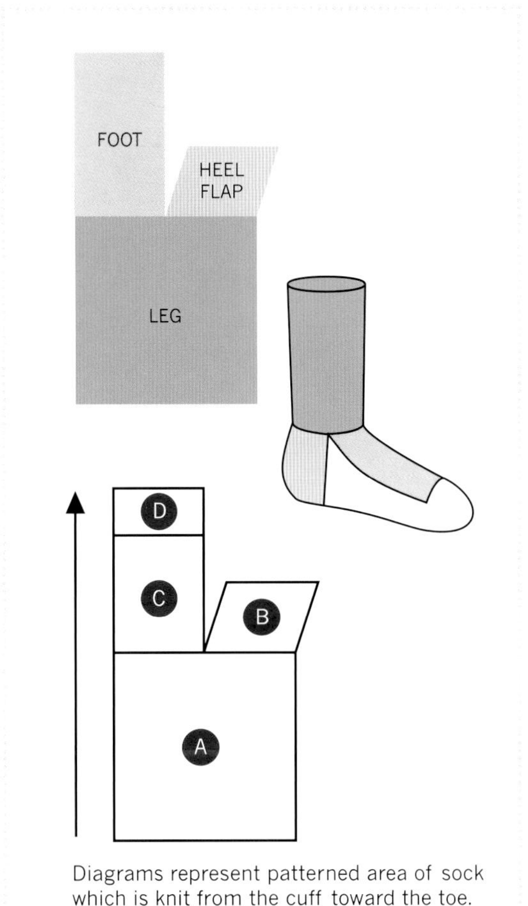

Diagrams represent patterned area of sock which is knit from the cuff toward the toe. Charts are worked as in diagram.

On right side: Slip 1 to cable needle and hold to back, k2 tbl from left needle, k1 from cable needle
On wrong side: Slip 2 to cable needle and hold to back, p1 from left needle, p2 tbl from cable needle

On right side: Slip 2 to cable needle and hold to front, k1 from left needle, k2 tbl from cable needle
On wrong side: Slip 1 to cable needle and hold to front, p2 tbl from left needle, p1 from cable needle

On right side: Slip 1 to cable needle and hold to back, k2 tbl from left needle, p1 from cable needle
On wrong side: Slip 2 to cable needle and hold to back, k1 from left needle, p2 tbl from cable needle

On right side: Slip 2 to cable needle and hold to front, p1 from left needle, k2 tbl from cable needle
On wrong side: Slip 1 to cable needle and hold to front, p2 tbl from left needle, k1 from cable needle

Slip 1 to cable needle and hold to back, k2 tbl from left needle, k1 tbl from cable needle

Slip 2 to cable needle and hold to front, k1 tbl from left needle, k2 tbl from cable needle

Slip 2 to cable needle and hold to back, k2 tbl from left needle, k2 tbl from cable needle

Slip 2 to cable needle and hold to front, k2 tbl from left needle, k2 tbl from cable needle

Slip 2 to cable needle and hold to back, k2 tbl from left needle, p2 from cable needle

Slip 2 to cable needle and hold to front, p2 from left needle, k2 tbl from cable needle

Slip 2 to cable needle and hold to back, k2tog tbl using one stitch from left needle and one stitch from cable needle—twice

On right side: Knit
On wrong side: Purl

On right side: Purl
On wrong side: Knit

On right side: Knit tbl
On wrong side: Purl tbl

On right side: K2tog
On wrong side: P2tog

On right side: Ssk
On wrong side: Ssp

Make 1

Knit into front, back, front of same stitch

Slip 1 with yarn held to wrong side

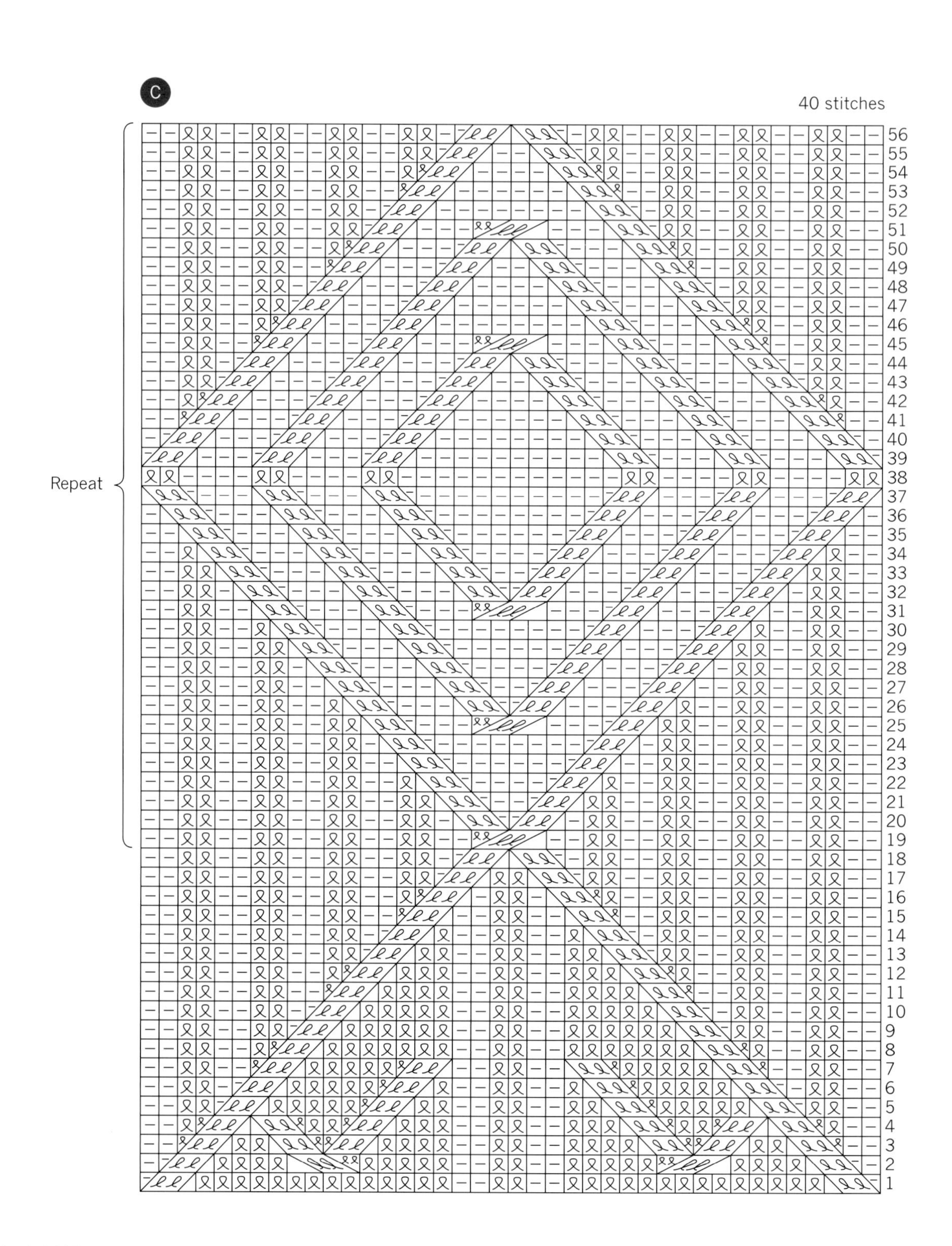
C
40 stitches
Repeat
56
55
54
53
52
51
50
49
48
47
46
45
44
43
42
41
40
39
38
37
36
35
34
33
32
31
30
29
28
27
26
25
24
23
22
21
20
19
18
17
16
15
14
13
12
11
10
9
8
7
6
5
4
3
2
1

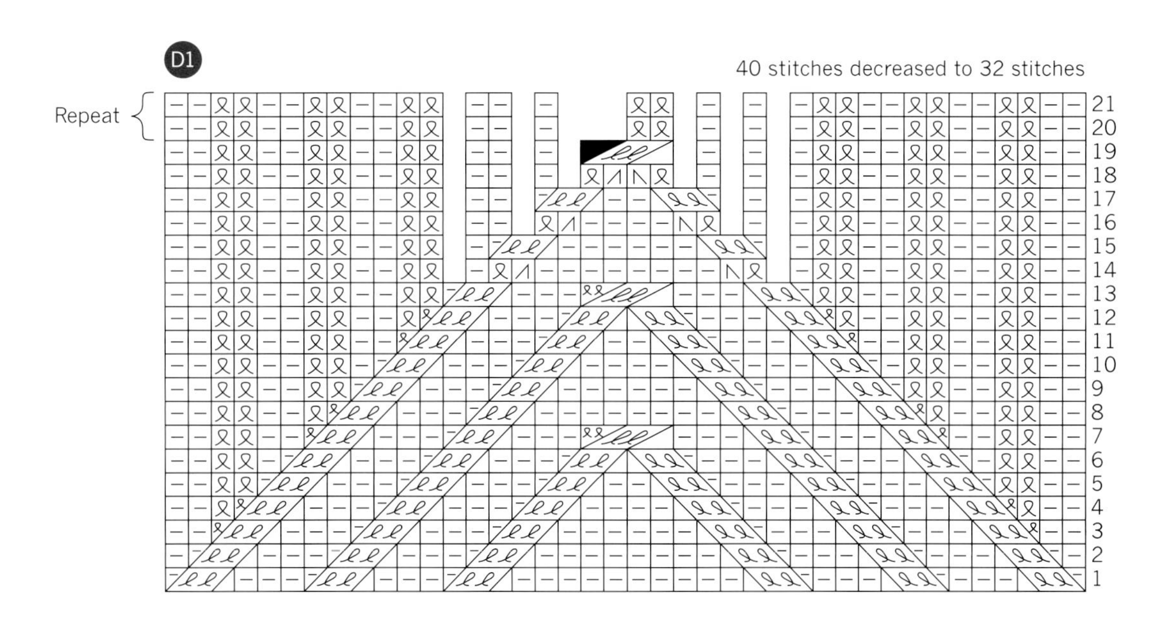
D1
40 stitches decreased to 32 stitches
Repeat
21
20
19
18
17
16
15
14
13
12
11
10
9
8
7
6
5
4
3
2
1

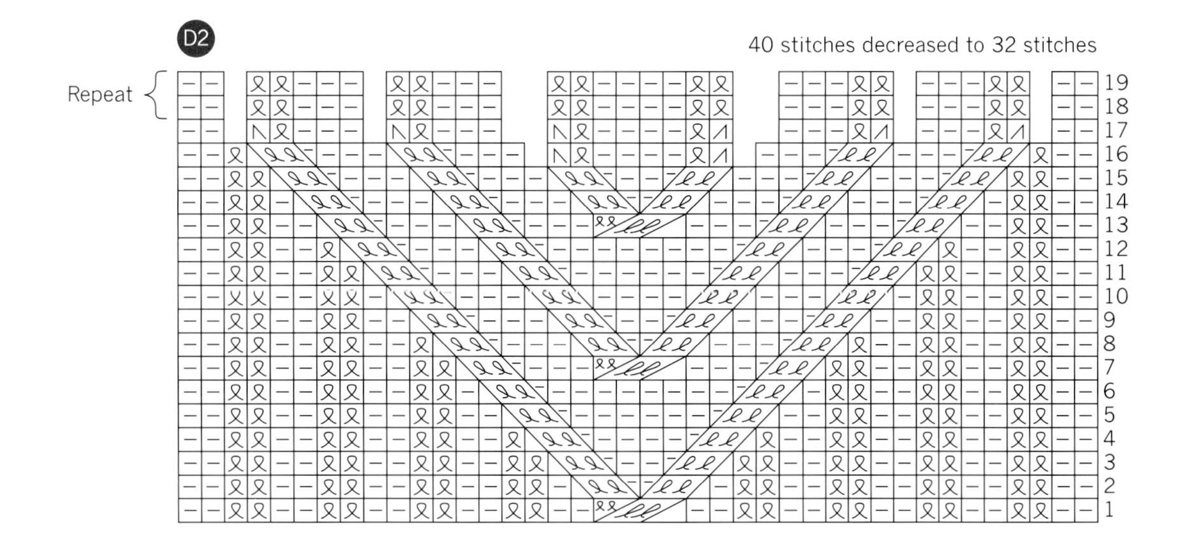
D2
40 stitches decreased to 32 stitches
Repeat
19
18
17
16
15
14
13
12
11
10
9
8
7
6
5
4
3
2
1

German Stockings

These knee high stockings feature twisted stitches in the traditional German style. Two panels emerge from a motif placed at the outer calf (right and left stockings are mirrored). Double twisted moss stitch grows between the two panels as one panel diverges from the other by traveling diagonally across the front of leg and top of the foot. A purl column carried down the back of the stockings creates a faux seam look.

O NOTES

Left and right socks are mirror images of each other. The diagrams on page 165 outline the construction and differences between the two versions. Both use charts A, B, and C on page 164. Directions are the same for both unless otherwise indicated. When two numbers are given, the first applies to the left sock with the number in brackets for the right sock.

Due to the extensive sizing of this pattern, numbers have been separated out into tables. Determine the numbers for your size on page 155 before beginning.

SIZE AND MEASUREMENTS

There are 5 foot sizes, **F1** to **F5**, that correspond to the foot circumference in the following table. Ankle circumference is the same as foot circumference.

There are 8 shaping sizes, **S1** to **S8**. Measure the widest circumference around your calf and use the following table to determine which shaping size to use. Negative ease of one to two inches is recommended.

		Foot Circ.	Shaping Size							
			S1	**S2**	**S3**	**S4**	**S5**	**S6**	**S7**	**S8**
Foot Size	**F1**	7"	10"	11"	12"	13"	14"	15"	16"	17"
	F2	8"	11"	12"	13"	14"	15"	16"	17"	18"
	F3	9"	12"	13"	14"	15"	16"	17"	18"	19"
	F4	10"	13"	14"	15"	16"	17"	18"	19"	20"
	F5	11"	14"	15"	16"	17"	18"	19"	20"	21"

SIZES
40 size combinations

Stockings shown are Foot Size 2 and Shaping Size 3

YARN
Shelridge Farm Soft Touch Ultra
100% wool
185 yards per 50g
3 to 5 skeins of Marigold
Size shown used 3 skeins

NEEDLES
US Size 1 / 2.25mm
or size needed to obtain gauge

NOTIONS
Cable needle, stitch markers, tapestry needle

GAUGE
In stockinette
32 stitches and 48 rows = 4"

In pattern
36 stitches and 48 rows = 4"

TABLES

Determine the numbers for your size combination using these tables.

Foot Size			Shaping Size							
			S1	S2	S3	S4	S5	S6	S7	S8
Foot Size	F1	a	66	74	82	90	98	106	114	122
		b	47	51	55	59	63	67	71	75
		c	18	22	26	30	34	38	42	46
		d	82	90	98	106	114	122	130	138
		e	10	14	18	22	26	30	34	38
	F2	a	74	82	90	98	106	114	122	130
		b	53	57	61	65	69	73	77	81
		c	20	24	28	32	36	40	44	48
		d	90	98	106	114	122	130	138	146
		e	12	16	20	24	28	32	36	40
	F3	a	82	90	98	106	114	122	130	138
		b	59	63	67	71	75	79	83	87
		c	22	26	30	34	38	42	46	50
		d	98	106	114	122	130	138	146	154
		e	14	18	22	26	30	34	38	42
	F4	a	90	98	106	114	122	130	138	146
		b	65	69	73	77	81	85	89	93
		c	24	28	32	36	40	44	48	52
		d	106	114	122	130	138	146	154	162
		e	16	20	24	28	32	36	40	44
	F5	a	98	106	114	122	130	138	146	154
		b	71	75	79	83	87	91	95	99
		c	26	30	34	38	42	46	50	54
		d	114	122	130	138	146	154	162	170
		e	18	22	26	30	34	38	42	46

	Foot Size				
	F1	**F2**	**F3**	**F4**	**F5**
f	13	17	21	25	29
g	14	16	18	20	22
h	58	66	74	82	90
i	29	33	37	41	45
j	15	17	19	21	23
k	17	19	21	23	25

	Shaping Size							
	S1	**S2**	**S3**	**S4**	**S5**	**S6**	**S7**	**S8**
l	12	16	14	10	6	2	0	0
m	0	0	6	14	22	30	36	40

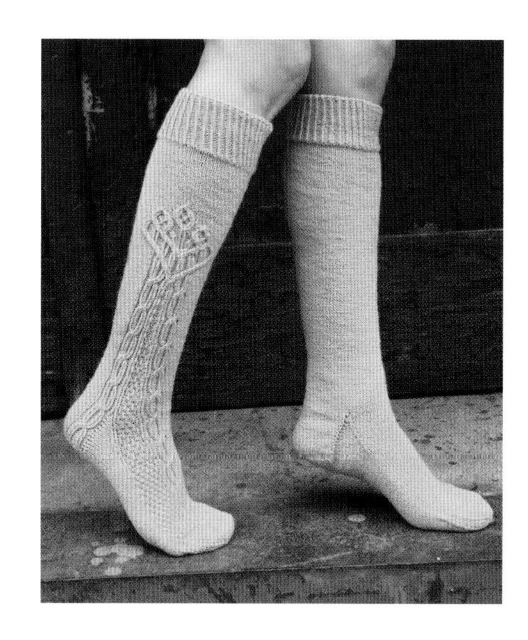

1 CUFF

Cast on **a** stitches. Being careful not to twist, join for working in the round and mark beginning of the round (page 168). (K1 tbl, p1) for 2 inches.

2 CALF SHAPING INCREASES

Right sock only Shift beginning of round one stitch to the left by knitting 1 stitch and marking new beginning of round.

Set-up Knit **b [c]** stitches, place marker, p1, knit to end of round.

Round 1 (Increase Round) Knit to 1 stitch before marker, make 1 right, k1, p1, k1, make 1 left, knit to end of round.

Round 2 (Even Round) Knit to marker, p1, knit to end of round.

Repeat last 2 rounds 7 more times. **d** stitches. Continue working even, without increasing, until piece measures 5 inches from cast-on edge.

3L LEG MOTIF – LEFT SOCK ONLY

Set-up Knit f stitches, place marker, k32, place marker, knit to marker, p1, knit to end of round.

Establish pattern Knit to marker, work chart A, work Calf Shaping Decrease Section (see sidebar) to end of round.

Continue established pattern through end of chart A.

3R LEG MOTIF – RIGHT SOCK ONLY

Set-up Knit to marker, p1, knit e stitches, place marker, knit to end of round.

Establish pattern Work Calf Shaping Decrease Section (see sidebar) to second marker, work chart A, knit to end of round.

Continue established pattern through end of chart A.

4L LEG TRAVELING PANELS – LEFT SOCK ONLY

Establish Traveling Panels and Double Twisted Moss Stitch as follows:

Set-up Knit to marker, remove marker, k4, k2tog, place marker, work chart B, place marker, make 1 left, place marker, work chart C, work Calf Shaping Decrease Section to end of round.

Round 1 (set round) Knit to marker, work chart B, work stitches as set (see sidebar) to marker, work chart C, work Calf Shaping Decrease Section to end of round.

Round 2 (opposite round) Knit to marker, work chart B, work stitches opposite as set (see sidebar) to marker, work chart C, work Calf Shaping Decrease Section to end of round.

Rounds 3 to 11 Alternate set round and opposite round for 9 more rounds.

Round 12 (Travel Round) Knit to 2 stitches before marker, k2tog, work chart B, slip marker, make 1 left in Double Twisted Moss Stitch (see sidebar), work stitches opposite as set to marker, work chart C, work Calf Shaping Decrease Section to end of round.

Repeat rounds 1 to 12, traveling every 12th round and continuing Calf Decrease Section, until sock measures 2¼ inches less than desired length from back of knee to floor. g stitches remain between purl column and end of round. h stitches.

CALF SHAPING DECREASE SECTION

Calf Shaping is worked at same time as Leg Motif and Traveling Panels (sections 3 and 4). Work decrease row every 4th row l times as follows.

Even rows Knit to marker, p1, knit to end of section.

Decrease row Knit to 2 stitches before marker, k2tog, p1, ssk, knit to end of section.

Then work decrease row every other row m times.

Then continue to work even without decreasing.

WORK STITCHES AS SET

Knit tbl the knit tbl's, and purl the purls.

WORK STITCHES OPPOSITE AS SET

Knit tbl the purls and make one purls, and purl the knit tbl's and make one knits.

MAKE 1 LEFT IN DOUBLE TWISTED MOSS STITCH

If the first stitch on the left needle is a knit tbl, then make 1 knit left. Otherwise, make 1 purl left.

MAKE 1 RIGHT IN DOUBLE TWISTED MOSS STITCH

If the last stitch worked was a knit tbl, then make 1 purl right. Otherwise, make 1 knit right.

4R LEG TRAVELING PANELS – RIGHT SOCK ONLY

Establish Traveling Panels and Double Twisted Moss Stitch as follows:

Set-up Work Calf Shaping Decrease Section to second marker, remove marker, k6, place marker, work chart B, place marker, make 1 right, place marker, work chart C, ssk, knit to end of round.

Round 1 (set round) Work Calf Shaping Decrease Section to second marker, work chart B, work stitches as set (see sidebar on page 159) to marker, work chart C, knit to end of round.

Round 2 (opposite round) Work Calf Shaping Decrease Section to second marker, work chart B, work stitches opposite as set (see sidebar on page 159) to marker, work chart C, knit to end of round.

Rounds 3 to 11 Alternate set round and opposite round for 9 more rounds.

Round 12 (Travel Round) Work Calf Shaping Decrease Section to second marker, work chart B, work stitches opposite as set to marker, make 1 right in Double Twisted Moss Stitch (see sidebar on page 159) before marker, work chart C, ssk, knit to end of round.

Repeat rounds 1 to 12, traveling every 12th round, while working Calf Shaping Decrease Section until sock measures 2¼ inches less than desired length from back of knee to floor. **g** stitches between beginning of round and purl column. **h** stitches total.

5L HEEL FLAP – LEFT SOCK ONLY

Divide for heel flap by placing next **i** stitches on hold for top of foot. Heel flap is worked back and forth over remaining **i** stitches. Turn work so that wrong side is facing.

Row 1 (wrong side) Slip 1 purlwise with yarn in front, purl to one stitch before marker, k1, purl to marker, work chart C except purl last stitch instead of purl tbl, turn.

Row 2 (right side) Slip 1 purlwise with yarn in back, work chart C, slip marker, knit to marker, p1, knit to end of row, turn.

Repeat last 2 rows until heel flap measures 2¼ inches, ending ready to work a right side row.

5R HEEL FLAP – RIGHT SOCK ONLY

Divide for heel flap by placing previous **i** stitches on hold for top of foot. Heel flap is worked back and forth over remaining **i** stitches .

Row 1 (right side) Slip 1 purlwise with yarn in back, knit to marker, p1, knit to marker, slip marker, work chart B except knit last stitch instead of knit tbl, turn.

Row 2 (wrong side) Slip 1 purlwise with yarn in front, work chart B, slip marker, purl to 1 stitch before marker, k1, slip marker, purl to end of row, turn.

Repeat last 2 rows until heel flap measures 2¼ inches, ending ready to work a right side row.

6 TURN HEEL

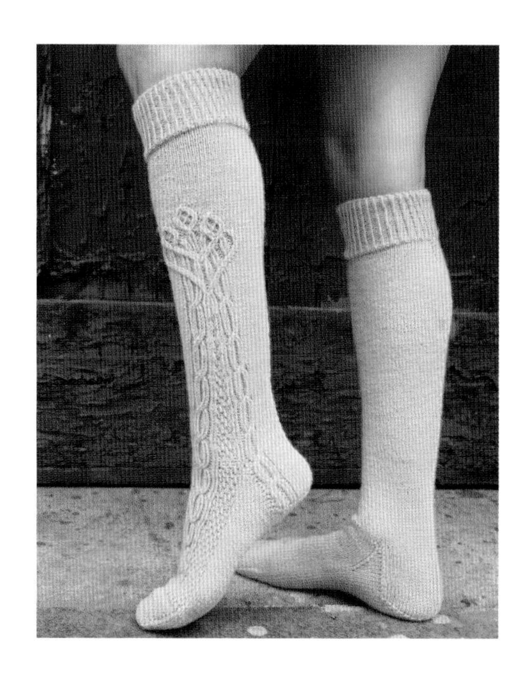

Continue working back and forth. Use short rows to turn heel as follows:

Row 1 (right side) Slip 1 purlwise with yarn in back, knit **j** stitches, ssk, k1, turn.

Row 2 (wrong side) Slip 1 purlwise with yarn in front, p4, p2tog, p1, turn.

Row 3 Slip 1 purlwise with yarn in back, knit to one stitch before gap caused by turn on previous row, ssk (using one stitch from each side of gap), k1, turn.

Row 4 Slip 1 purlwise with yarn in front, purl to one stitch before gap caused by turn on previous row, p2tog (using one stitch from each side of gap), p1, turn.

Repeat last 2 rows until all heel stitches have been worked, ending ready to work a right side row. **k** heel stitches.

7 FOOT

Resume working in the round as follows: Slip 1 purlwise with yarn in back, knit approximately halfway across heel and mark beginning of round. Knit remaining heel stitches, pick up and knit into each slipped stitch along edge of heel flap, make 1, mark right side of foot, continue established pattern across held stitches, mark left side of foot, make 1, pick up and knit into each slipped stitch along edge of heel flap, knit to end of round.

Right and left side markers divide foot into top of foot section (previously held stitches) and sole. Decrease 2 sole stitches every other round as follows:

Round 1 Knit to 2 stitches before right side of foot, k2tog, work established pattern (continue traveling every 12th round) to left side of foot, ssk, knit to end of round. 2 stitches decreased.

Round 2 Knit to right side of foot, work established pattern to left side of foot, knit to end of round.

Repeat last 2 rounds until **h** stitches remain.

Continue working even, without decreasing sole stitches, until foot measures 2 inches less than desired length from back of heel turn. If chart C [B] reaches side of foot, continue in established pattern across top of foot without traveling.

8 TOE

Knit to right side of foot. This is the new beginning of round.

Round 1 Knit to end of round.

Round 2 K1, ssk, knit to 3 stitches before left side of foot, k2tog, k2 (one stitch before and one stitch after left side of foot marker), ssk, knit to 3 stitches before right side of foot, k2tog, k1. 4 stitches decreased.

Repeat last 2 rounds until foot measures desired length, ending after a decrease round. Graft top of foot stitches to sole stitches using Kitchener stitch (page 167). Weave in ends and block.

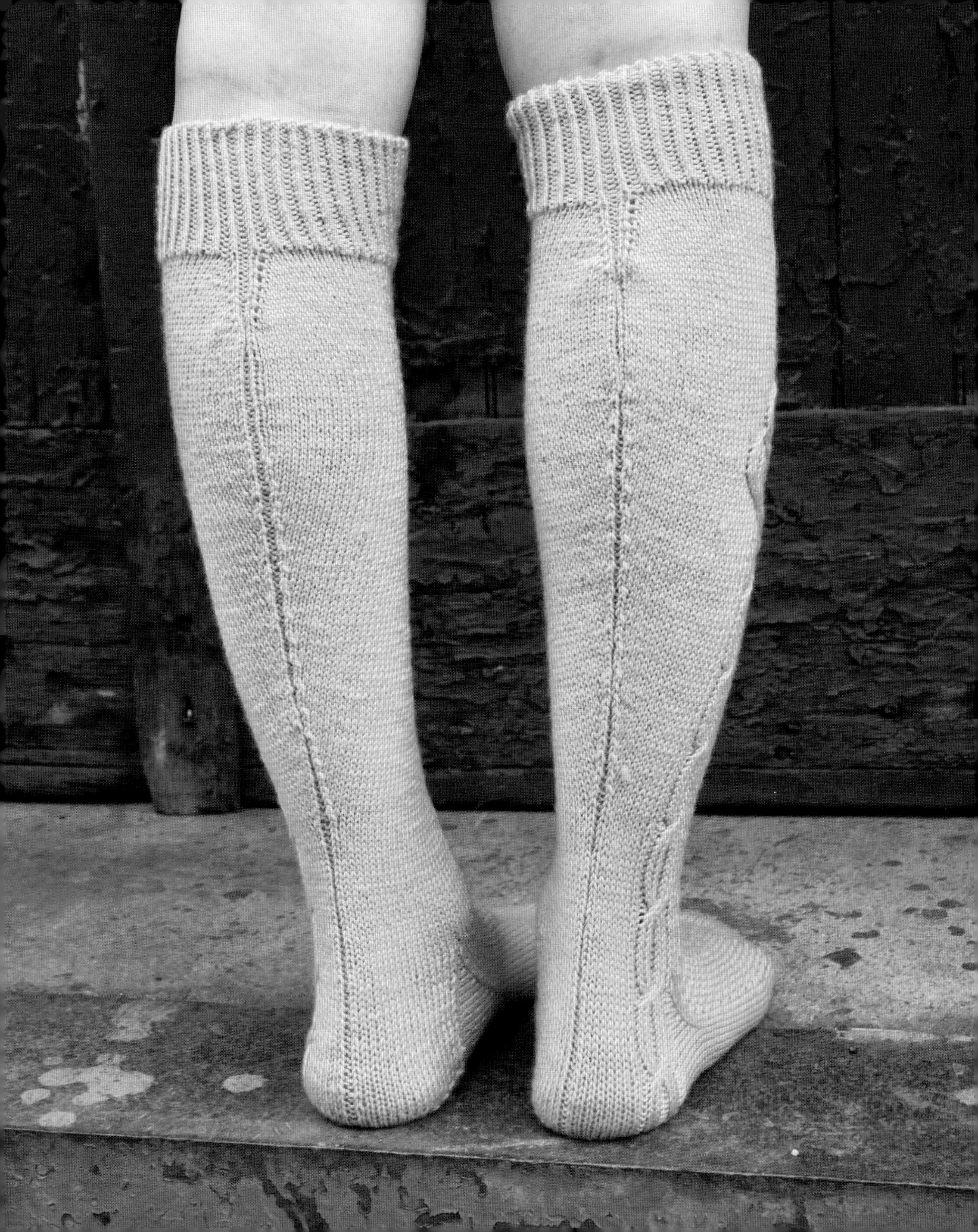

C — 10 stitches

Rows: 12, 11, 10, 9, 8, 7, 6, 5, 4, 3, 2, 1

B — 10 stitches

Rows: 12, 11, 10, 9, 8, 7, 6, 5, 4, 3, 2, 1

A — 32 stitches

Rows: 36, 35, 34, 33, 32, 31, 30, 29, 28, 27, 26, 25, 24, 23, 22, 21, 20, 19, 18, 17, 16, 15, 14, 13, 12, 11, 10, 9, 8, 7, 6, 5, 4, 3, 2, 1

- On right side: Knit
  On wrong side: Purl
- On right side: Purl
  On wrong side: Knit
- On right side: Knit tbl
  On wrong side: Purl tbl
- Slip 1 to cable needle and hold to back, k1 tbl from left needle, k1 tbl from cable needle
- Slip 1 to cable needle and hold to front, k1 tbl from left needle, knit 1 tbl from cable needle
- Slip 1 to cable needle and hold to back, k1 tbl from left needle, p1 from cable needle
- Slip 1 to cable needle and hold to front, p1 from left needle, k1 tbl from cable needle
- Slip 1 to cable needle and hold to back, k2 tbl from left needle, k1 from cable needle
- Slip 2 to cable needle and hold to front, k1 from left needle, k2 tbl from cable needle
- Slip 1 to cable needle and hold to back, k2 tbl from left needle, p1 from cable needle
- Slip 2 to cable needle and hold to front, p1 from left needle, k2 tbl from cable needle
- Slip 1 to cable needle and hold to back, k2 tbl from left needle, k1 tbl from cable needle
- Slip 2 to cable needle and hold to front, k1 tbl from left needle, k2 tbl from cable needle
- On right side: Slip 2 to cable needle and hold to back, k2 tbl from left needle, k2 tbl from cable needle
  On wrong side: Slip 2 to cable needle and hold to back, p2 tbl from left needle, p2 tbl from

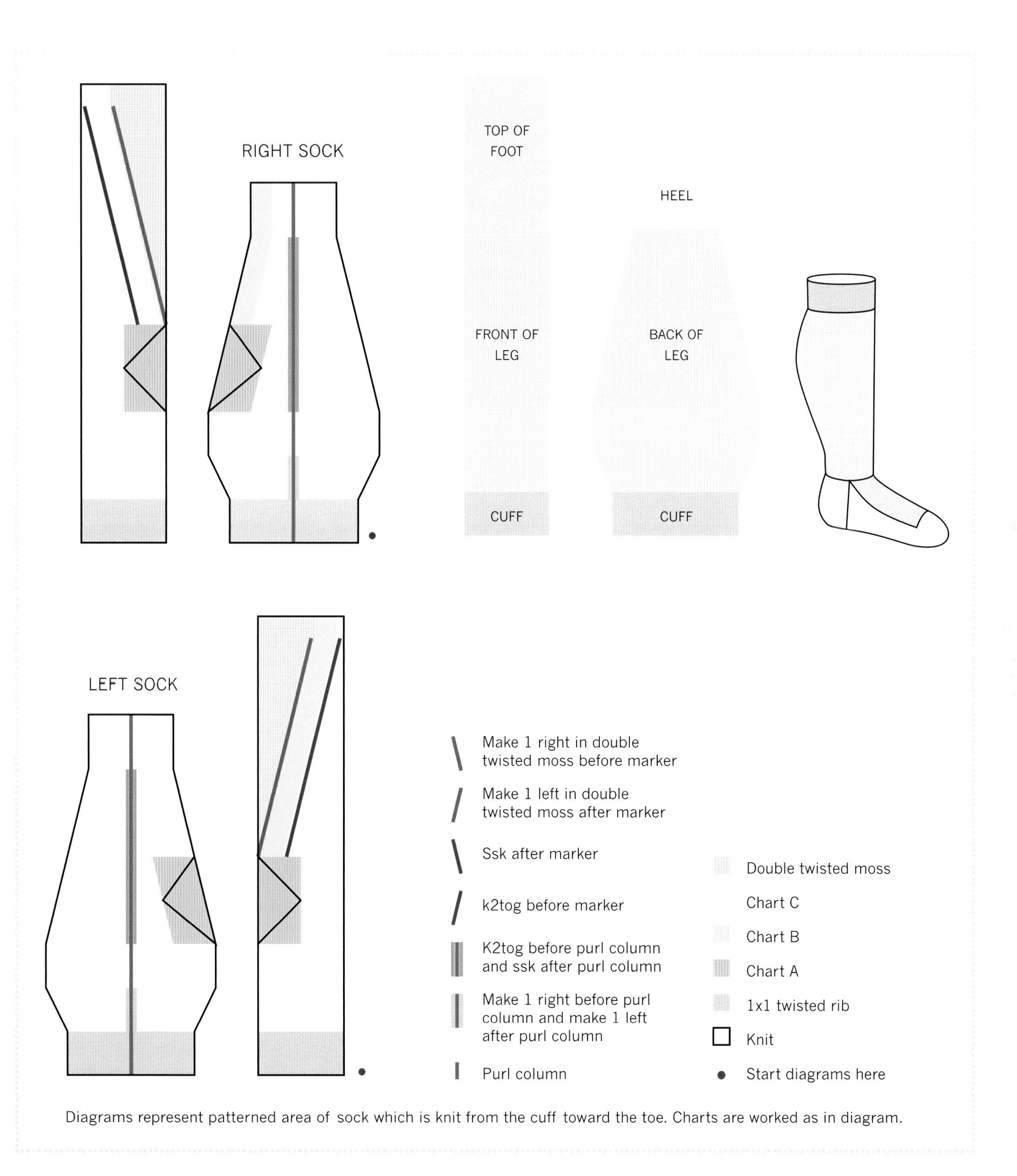

Diagrams represent patterned area of sock which is knit from the cuff toward the toe. Charts are worked as in diagram.

ABBREVIATIONS AND TERMS

k knit

p purl

k2tog knit 2 together

k3tog knit 3 together

p2tog purl 2 together

ssk slip 2 stitches knitwise individually, insert left needle into 2 slipped stitches through the front, knit the 2 slipped stitches together through the back loop from this position

sssk slip 3 stitches knitwise individually, insert left needle into 3 slipped stitches through the front, knit the 3 slipped stitches together through the back loop from this position

ssp slip 2 stitches knitwise individually, pass slipped stitches purlwise back to left needle, purl 2 slipped stitches together through the back loop

tbl through back loop

yo yarnover

make 1, make 1 knit, make 1 knit left (all the same)
pick up bar of yarn between the needles from the front with the left needle, knit the newly picked up stitch through the back loop

make 1 right, make 1 knit right (both the same)
pick up bar of yarn between the needles from the back with the left needle, knit the newly picked up stitch through the front loop

make 1 purl, make 1 purl right (both the same)
pick up bar of yarn between the needles from the back with the left needle, purl the newly picked up stitch

make 1 purl left
pick up bar of yarn between the needles from the front with the left needle, purl the newly picked up stitch through the back loop

wrap and turn
With yarn in back of work, slip the next stitch purlwise, bring working yarn to front of the work, and slip the slipped stitch from the right needle back to the left needle without changing its orientation. Turn work so opposite side is now facing with wrapped stitch on the right needle.

Kitchener stitch
Divide stitches evenly between two needles held parallel to each other with both tips facing right and last stitch worked as the rightmost stitch on the back needle. For all patterns in this book, stitches on the front needle will be the half from the top of the foot while the stitches on the back needle will be the toe stitches from the sole. Cut working yarn, leaving a two foot tail, and thread through a tapestry needle. Graft stitches together, from right to left, by working steps 1 through 6 once, then repeating steps 3 through 6 until 2 stitches remain—one on each needle, then working steps 3 and 5 to finish off last two stitches.

1. Insert tapestry needle into first stitch on front needle purlwise and pull yarn through while leaving stitch on needle.
2. Insert tapestry needle into first stitch on back needle knitwise and pull yarn through while leaving stitch on needle.
3. Insert tapestry needle into first stitch on front needle knitwise, pull yarn through, and drop that stitch from the needles.
4. Insert tapestry needle through next stitch on front needle purlwise and pull yarn through while leaving stitch on needle.
5. Insert tapestry needle into first stitch on back needle purlwise, pull yarn through, and drop that stitch from the needles.
6. Insert tapestry needle through next stitch on back needle knitwise and pull yarn through while leaving stitch on needle.

General Information

WORKING IN THE ROUND

Cast on

I prefer a long tail cast-on, but any cast on that is loose and stretchy will suffice for socks. The patterns in this book are written generically for any type of needles: 4 or 5 double pointed needles or 1 or 2 circular needles. Divide the cast-on stitches among the needles as specified in the pattern.

Shifting the beginning of the round

Many patterns call for shifting the beginning of the round. After shifting the beginning of the round, also shift the stitches among the other needles so that each needle has a multiple of the number of stitches in the pattern repeat.

Markers for beginning of round and sides of the foot

Markers for the beginning of round, right side of foot, and left side of foot are referred to in the patterns but stitch markers are not necessary. These placements can be marked with the needles by arranging the stitches such that each placement occurs between needle changes or where the cord twists when working with one circular needle. If working with circular needles, a marker may be used to mark the beginning of the round on the foot but is not necessary if you remember that the beginning of the round always occurs at the middle of the sole and then later shifts to the right side of the foot before working the toe. The exact location of the beginning of the round during the foot is not important.

WORKING FROM CHARTS AND DIAGRAMS

Charts

Always begin charts at the bottom and work upwards, just like the piece is knitted. Read each right side row from right to left. When on the wrong side, such as on a heel flap, read the row from left to right using the wrong side directions for each symbol. Row numbers indicate the beginning of each row: when the row number is on the right, it is a right side row that is to be worked from right to left; when the row number is on the left, it is a wrong side row that is to be worked from left to right. Because charts are worked from the bottom up, charts are often arranged throughout the book with the first chart used within a pattern at the lower right of the page or spread.

Diagrams

Diagrams represent the patterned portion of each sock. When working in the round from a diagram, work from the bottom and right to left, similarly to charts.

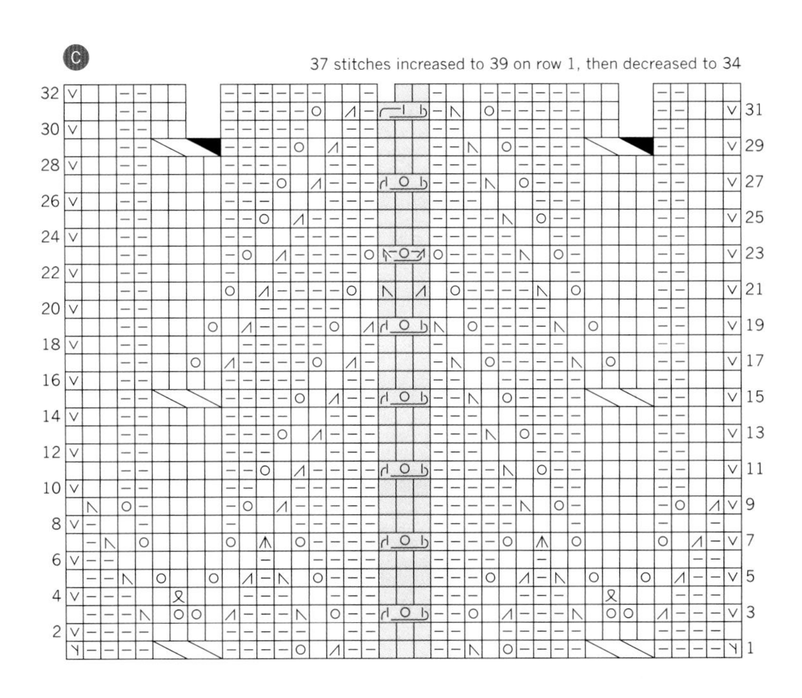

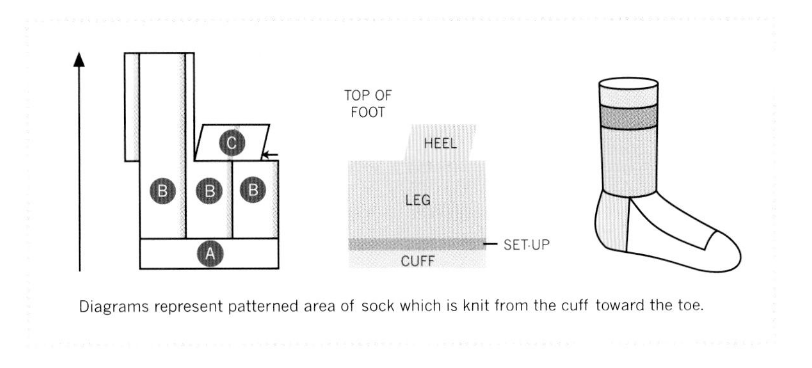

Diagrams represent patterned area of sock which is knit from the cuff toward the toe.

Resources

ONLINE HELP

If you're unsure about a certain technique, there are many sources for help online. Here are recommended websites.

Knitter's Review
www.knittersreview.com
Impartial reviews of yarns, tools, and books. Weekly newsletter filled with information and events listings.

Knitty
www.knitty.com
Free online magazine with technique articles featuring clear photographs demonstrating how to knit in the round and how to pick up stitches.

Ravelry
www.ravelry.com
The forums on the Ravelry website are invaluable. Join the *Cookie's Socks* group and connect with thousands of knitters.

BOOKS

As a book learner, I prefer to consult books when I have questions. Here is some suggested reading.

Getting Started Knitting Socks
by Ann Budd
A great introduction to sock knitting if you've never done it before.

Sock Innovation: Knitting Techniques and Patterns for One-of-a-Kind Socks
by Cookie A
Information on how to design your own socks as well as a glossary illustrating some sock techniques.

Knitter's Handbook: A Comprehensive Guide to the Principles and Techniques of Handknitting
by Montse Stanley
An all-purpose knitting reference that no knitter should be without.

YARNS

The yarns in this book were generously provided by the following yarn companies. Visit their websites to find a stockist near you.

Blue Moon Fiber Arts
www.bluemoonfiberarts.com

Cascade Yarns
www.cascadeyarns.com

Claudia Hand Painted Yarns
www.claudiaco.com

Dream in Color Yarns
www.dreamincoloryarn.com

Hand Jive Knits
www.handjiveknits.com

Hazel Knits
www.hazelknits.com

Koigu Wool Designs
www.koigu.com

Lorna's Laces
www.lornaslaces.net

Louet North America
www.louet.com

Malabrigo Yarn
www.malabrigoyarn.com

Pagewood Farm
www.pagewoodfarm.com

Shelridge Farm
www.shelridge.com

Skacel Collections
www.skacelknitting.com

DREAM

Credits

STYLIST

SARAH BEAVER is a trained art conservator with an immense love of all-things related to the history of fashion and cinema. Working within the realm of aesthetics, be it architectural conservation or wardrobe styling, is what helps to keep her feeling engaged. This book contains her first published styling work to date. She hopes to continue to be able to work in fields that create and preserve beauty all through life.

MODELS

MERCEDES AVERY is a passionate woman who loves life, deeply cares about people and wishes to make a difference. Her frank honesty and straightforward, outspoken ways often get her into trouble with her friends, but they love her anyway!

CHLOE BARCELOU remains enigmatic.

GENEVIEVE BURKE is a graduate of Temple University in Philadelphia. Her clients have included the Art Institute of Philadelphia, Bloomingdales, Interweave Knits, Neiman Marcus, Urban Outfitters and Warsaw Made.

MARLO MEEKINS is an artist whose paintings have earned her a cult following and clients such as Jack Black and Nickelodeon. She also models, knits, sews, sings and cooks as divine forms of procrastination. See her work at MarloMeekins.blogspot.com

TANYA DAKIN modeled socks for the close-up detail photos. Her feet are perfect.

Hot coals, 2009

Credits

SAMPLE AND TEST KNITTERS

BFF

Jessica Dekker
Denise DeSantis
Annmarie Fumicello
Salla Matkaselkä
Dianne Pearson
Chelsea Welp

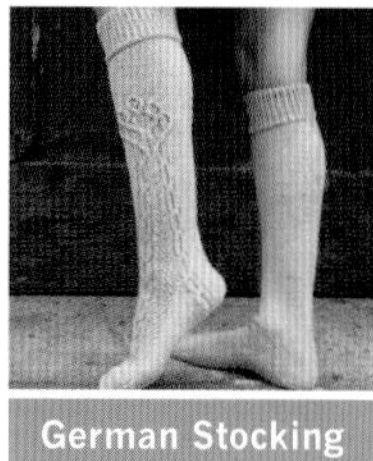

German Stocking

Jeanette Robinson
Kristy Boyer
Ceylan Gul
Deb Jaworowicz
Louise Mutterperl
Monica Nappe
Leslie Thompson

Lissajous sock

Barbara Mellert
Katie Kearney
Bobbi Kraft
Michelle Logsdon

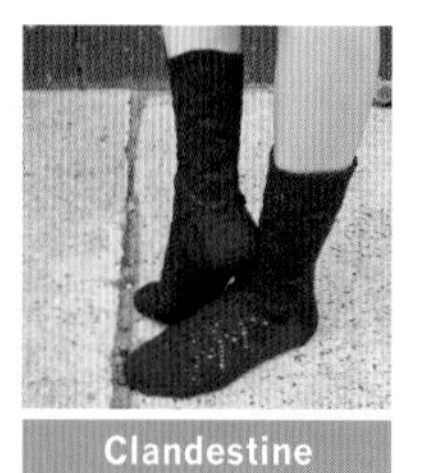

Clandestine

Barbara Mellert
Tamara Johnston
Tara Smith
Caroline Wright

Gothic Spire

Christine Craig
Rayleen Burnett
Hillary Rubin
Susan Smith
Heather Storta

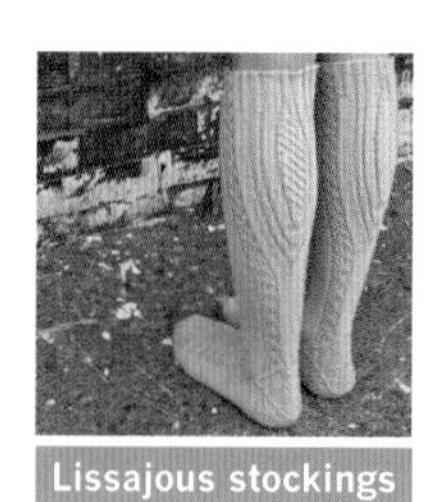

Lissajous stockings

Hattie Adkins
Jana Anell
Hannah Ball
Cathie Botts
Amy Machael

Cusp

Alyson Johnson
Laura Beutler
Martha Friedman
Becca Huben
Sarah Lehto
Kate LePore
Lindsay Mabe
Denise Montague
Anastasia Rynearson
Molly Sherwood
Stephanie Vianelli-Nixon
Koren A. Wake

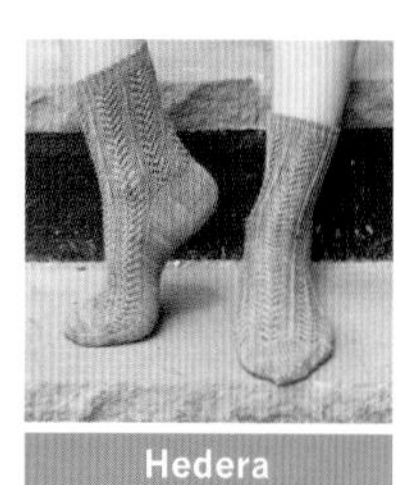

Hedera

Amy Palmer
Ellen Gowey
Celia Jones
Erna Klüver
Amy Machael
Kimberly Roy
Sarah Selli

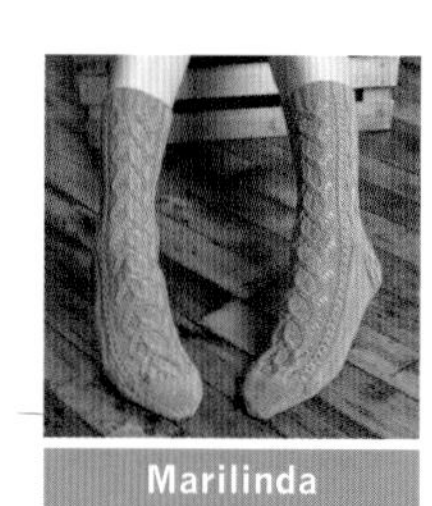

Marilinda

Jackie Dyer
Rachel Peck
Faythe Saxton
Chrysoula Tzavelas
Ana Wismer

In and Out

Cheryl Litt
Melissa Bethel
Judi Chandler
Nathalie Hall
Jessie Hergenrader
Kristin Marciniak
Shayla McConnell

Mona

Lynn Hall
Beth Comstock
Susan Ginnings
N Ran-Santos

Monkey

Julie Bernhardt
Amy Machael
Bethany Niebauer
Melissa Tuttle Sibley

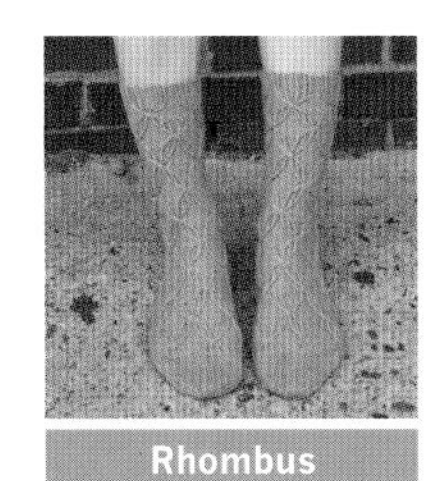

Rhombus

Eva Sweeney
Sarah Cline
Carol Macke
Paula McKeever
Jaya Purswani
Tia Weinand

Thelonious

Sarah Earle
Heidi Kirsch
Celia McCuaig
Deirdre McNeill
Dianne Peterson

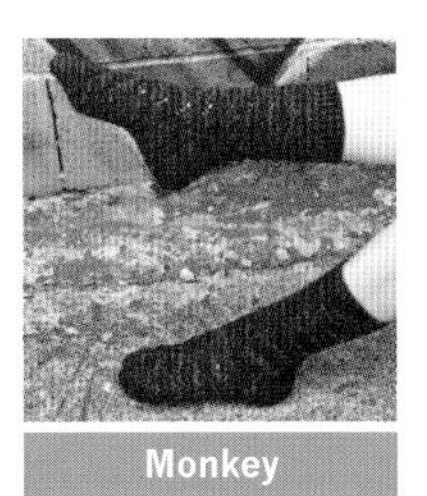

Monkey

Barbara Mellert

Sake

Jeannie Cartmel
Carla Bell
Candice Clifford
Christi Dillon
Nanette Donohue
Brenda Stevens

Twisted Flower

Jolene Lau
Jennifer Curry
Thuy Le
Kelly Nelsen

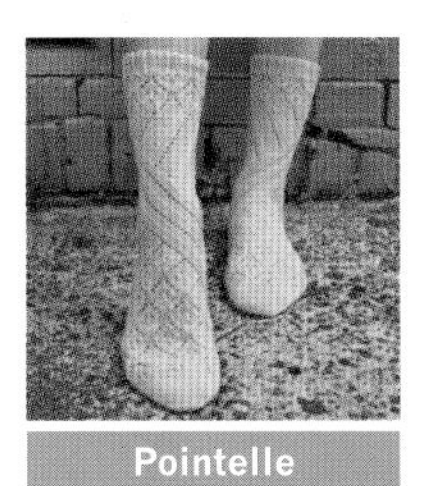

Pointelle

Debbie O'Neill
Yvonne Eyer
Lise Hymel
Susan Lutsky
Dana Matthews
Lisa McKean
Anne Schroeder

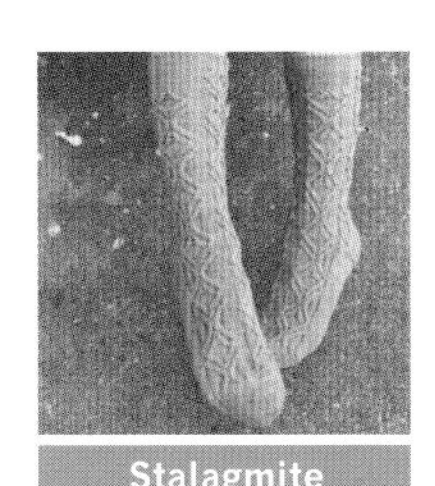

Stalagmite

Monica Nappe
Malia Arguello
Rachel Atkinson
Margaret Bonifer
Beck Gusler
Mairead McGrath

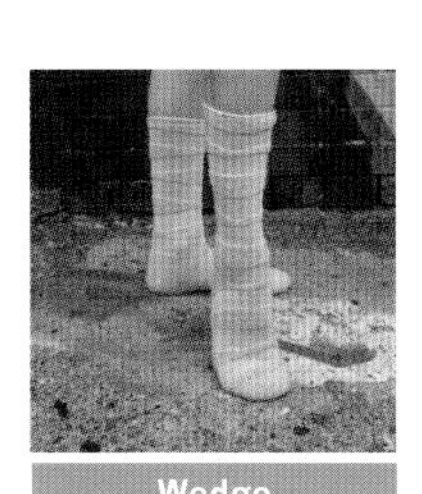

Wedge

Caryn Lantz
Michelle Dyck
Kate Fuhrman
Heather Jacobsen
Michele Ziemer

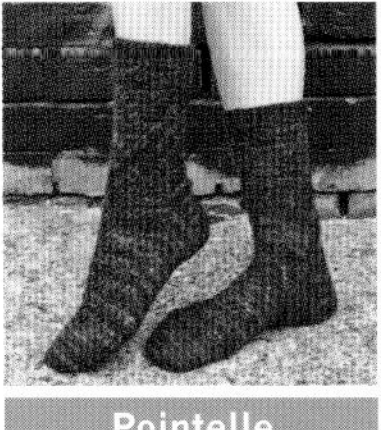

Pointelle

Hattie Adkins

Stricken

Jaya Purswani
Suzanne Boswell
Jeannie Cartmel
Hannah Denney
Madeleine Fitzgerald
Kathy Parker
Amber Pulley
Penny Tallman

Wedge

Celia McCuaig

Acknowledgments

I have many people to thank for making this book possible. Most of all, I would like to thank my husband who has been amazingly supportive. He provided fresh insight at so many steps along the way despite having never knit a stitch in his life. I'm grateful that my parents instilled in me the sometimes unrealistic notion that I can do anything if I just work hard enough. And special thanks to Kristi Geraci for convincing me to begin knitting socks in the first place. I don't know what I would be doing now otherwise.

I've gotten to know many people through working on this book, many of whom have contributed directly. A huge thanks to Laura Kicey for her stunning photography, Sarah Beaver for the styling, and the models for beautifully showcasing the socks. Vanessa Yap-Einbund's simple and elegant layout and design aesthetic adds wonderfully subtle details to the presentation of the patterns. Janice Kang's meticulous technical editing and patience went above and beyond the call of duty. I give an especially heartfelt thanks to the sample knitters who gave my ideas actual physical shape, the numerous knitters who tested these patterns to ensure they are as error-free as possible, and the yarn companies who generously provided materials.

The knitting community has been absolutely wonderful and there are many knitters to whom I am grateful for paving the way and providing support: Amy Singer and *Knitty.com* for giving me the invaluable opportunity to share my work with so many knitters, Cat Bordhi for her sage advice from a lifetime of experience and for organizing the immensely supportive and knowledgeable Visionary group, Janel Laidman for spending countless hours day and night discussing all things knitting related with me and keeping me going through the final days, Anne Hanson for letting me bake at her house and always providing a fresh and honest point of view, Chris DeLongpre for much needed advice early on, and Jared Flood for inspiring me to make the world a more beautiful place.

And I would like to thank you, dear reader, for picking up this book. I hope you enjoy knitting socks as much as I do.